Mozart

*A Meditation on His Life
and Mysterious Death*

by Dr. Stefan Carter

Heartland Associates, Inc.
Winnipeg, Canada

Printed in Manitoba, Canada

CREDITS

EDITOR Barbara Huck
ASSOCIATE EDITOR Peter St. John
MAPS, DESIGN & LAYOUT Dawn Huck
IMAGE RESEARCH Lindsay Lovallo
PRINTING Friesens

Library and Archives Canada Cataloguing in Publication

Carter, Stefan, 1928-
        Mozart: a meditation on his life and mysterious death/Stefan
Carter.

ISBN 1-896150-25-X (bound)
ISBN 1-896150-37-3 (pbk.)

        1. Mozart, Wolfgang Amadeus, 1756-1791. 2. Composers--Austria--
Biography. I. Title.

ML410.M9C325 2005   780'.92   C2005-907093-5

Front cover: Original image by Joshua Stanton

Back cover: Salzburg's Old City, a World Heritage Site,
courtesy of Tourismus Salzburg GmbH

 Conseil des Arts   Canada Council
du Canada   for the Arts

Mozart

*A Meditation on His Life
and Mysterious Death*

by Dr. Stefan Carter

Dedication

This book is dedicated to the memory of my parents
Janina and Waclaw Reicher
and to my aunt and uncle
Stanislawa and Maksymilian Centnerszwer,
all artists who perished in the Holocaust.

TABLE OF CONTENTS

Music flowed from Mozart's mind like water from a fountain, but even he found the process of writing it down for performance, publication, or posterity tiresome.

IMAGNO/Austrian Archives

ACKNOWLEDGEMENTS

I wish to acknowledge the immensely important influence and assistance of Doctor Kurt Markstrom of the University of Manitoba's Faculty of Music, who reignited my interest in Mozart's life, encouraged me, and selflessly helped in my endeavours. I received valuable assistance from other members of the faculty, as well as from from librarians Sonja Paas and Marc Rabnett of the university's Carolyn Sifton-Helen Fuld Library; Sonja and the late Gerhard Labies also provided help with translations from German sources. Professor Peter St. John, a senior scholar at the U of M, read the original manuscript and provided several important suggestions. The staff at Heartland Associates expertly steered the work to its final form and the input of Barbara Huck breathed fresh spirit into the manuscript that helped it come alive.

I would also like to acknowledge the members of my family to whom this book is dedicated, who sowed the seeds of my lifelong interest in music. My mother, Janina Reicher, studied and taught music. I remember her playing the music of Chopin and Beethoven, as well as chamber music, with my father Waclaw Reicher, an amateur violinist, and others when I was a youngster. I was taught music in school by my uncle, Maksymilian Centnerszwer, a professional musician, pedagogue and composer, whose works were performed by the Warsaw Philharmonic Orchestra before World War II. His wife, Stanislawa Centnerszwer was a well-known and prolific painter. They all perished in the Holocaust.

Dr. Stefan A. Carter
October 2005

PREFACE

On New Year's Eve 2001, exhilarated by the wondrous experience of learning more about Mozart and his music after auditing a course at the University of Manitoba's Faculty of Music, I decided to continue this fascinating journey by examining what we know about the composer nearly 250 years after he was born. It seemed the perfect time to embark on this voyage of discovery. As I looked skyward at midnight, I could see the planet Jupiter directly overhead. The last time it was overhead at midnight on a New Year's Eve was in 1752. Leopold and Maria Anna Mozart were then enjoying life in Salzburg with their infant daughter "Nannerl", and Wolfgang Amadeus Mozart was not even a gleam in his father's eye.

Since then, I have discovered many differing views about Mozart and his life; this book is an attempt to analyze and compare those ideas. I hope this 'Mozart Primer' may be of interest to readers who wish to learn more about the composer and his music, and to students embarking on a career in music. This work is based on primary sources I consulted either in the original German or in translation, and on many secondary sources, including several prominent biographies that appeared in the early 1990s, around the time of the 200th anniversary of Mozart's death. From these, I have attempted to summarize the events of his life and his oeuvre, and to outline, as much as possible, an image of a man whose music continues to touch and fascinate millions. My sources are listed in the bibliography and may be consulted by readers who wish to continue the search.

Part I presents a chronology of the composer's life, and looks briefly at his family after his death. Sections on his compositions may be of particular interest to those whose passion is his music; however seeing them in context, woven into the story of his life, will—I hope—also enlighten those who are primarily interested in Mozart, the man. Mozart's compositions are identified chronologically by a "K" number according to a catalogue first published in 1862 by a scholar, Ludwig Ritter von Köchel, which has since undergone several revisions.

Part II deals with the composer's personality, health, social and financial matters, and the relationships within the Mozart family. Part III is concerned with Mozart's musicianship, its development, his compositional output, and the perception of his music by other musicians during his lifetime and thereafter.

The appendices provide a list of fifty arbitrarily chosen masterpieces, and a short glossary of musical terms that might be helpful to those without grounding in music theory.

Introduction

Wolfgang Amadeus Mozart, who has been called the world's greatest composer, lived during the second half of the eighteenth century in the Holy Roman Empire. Beginning in 1438, the empire had been ruled, with few interruptions, by members of the Germanic Hapsburg dynasty, mainly from their Imperial Court in Vienna. For centuries, the Hapsburgs had been able to protect the empire's loose federation of member states from external threats and internal strife. Otherwise, the states enjoyed relative autonomy and were ruled by the electors, both secular and religious. Among the latter were the Archbishops of Salzburg.

Nestled along a curve of the Salzach River in what is now north-western Austria, Salzburg has many reasons to be proud of its past. This is an ancient place, with roots that go back at least 4,000 years. Its cultural foundations are buttressed by Celtic, Roman, Frankish, Bavarian and Austrian contributions, while its religious life has included Catholic, Jewish and Protestant influences. But Salzburg is perhaps best known for its music. Its geographical location, on the northern boundary of the Alps, and its long history as an ecclesiastical principality combined to make it a place of musical renown greatly out of proportion to its size. Foremost among its musical claims to fame is the subject of this book, Wolfgang Mozart. "Wolferl", as the locals called him, creator of music that has been described as nothing short of heavenly.

Salzburg's origins lie with something far more down to earth, however. We may never know who first discovered the "white gold" of the mountains that gave the river, the town and the province their names, and the community its considerable wealth and power, but the mining of the region's deep deposits of salt, or *salz*, goes back thousands of years. The first neolithic—or perhaps even paleolithic—inhabitants lived in mountain caves, but as time passed, Celtic settlements grew up along the river near the mines. Then, just over two thousand years ago, the Romans merged these riverside settlements into a town called Juva-vum, which became an important regional hub.

Eighteenth century Salzburg lithograph by Figenthum d. Verleger

After the collapse of the Roman Empire, the town dwindled until, sometime in the late fifth century, an early Christian community was founded by a monk named St. Severin. Some 200 years later, the old monastery was rebuilt and a church was created, marking the beginning of the modern city of Salzburg. In 798, at the request of the Emperor Charlemagne, the town was designated an archbishopric, with influence over other, older Bavarian dioceses. As the centuries passed, Salzburg became an ecclesiastical principality, ruled by a prince-archbishop, with the exclusive privilege of being directly responsible to the emperor. This remarkable influence, which was secular as well as religious, lasted for centuries, until the end of the Holy Roman Empire in 1806.

The successive archbishops were certainly not all compassionate men. They were powerful and often ruthless, but on two things many agreed: the creation of a city of baroque majesty, and the nurturing and support of a musical legacy. Through the seventeenth and eighteenth centuries, successive archbishops embarked on major building programs in what is now known as the Old City; all told, more than 100 churches, castles and palaces stand witness to the power and imagination of the archbishops. In 1997, to protect this cultural legacy, UNESCO named Salzburg's Old City a World Heritage Site.

Many of the archbishops also encouraged and funded music, both religious and secular, employing a Kappelmeister and Vice-Kappelmeister, as well as musicians, composers and singers. Situated on a natural thoroughfare 150 kilometres east of Munich and 300 kilometres west of Vienna, Salzburg enjoyed musical talent from both west and east, and a reputation for excellence and innovation that far outreached its size. But as this book explains, the city's most significant and best-known citizen felt forced to leave in order to escape the constraints the last of the archbishops placed on him. Nevertheless, Mozart continues to be much celebrated in his birthplace and his earliest home, at No. 9 Getreidegasse, has been painstakingly refurbished. Today it attracts flocks of admirers and devotees. The city also boasts plazas in Mozart's name and statues that recall his enormous contribution to music worldwide.

Mozart was not alone in creating Salzburg's musical legacy.

This was also the birthplace of Josef Mohr. Working with composer Franz Gruber, Mohr, who wrote the text, created the world's pre-eminent anthem of Christmas, "Silent Night", which was first performed in 1818. And since the end of the nineteenth century, the celebrated Salzburg Festival has drawn many of the world's great composers and conductors to a pageant of music and drama held for five weeks each summer. Another draw, particularly for North Americans, is visiting the various sites that were featured in the *Sound of Music*. The enormously popular film, which was based on the true story of a Salzburg nun who saved an aristocratic family from Nazi forces, was shot in and around Salzburg in 1964.

In 1756, the year of Mozart's birth, the overwhelming majority of people of the empire, as well as of other European countries, were abjectly poor; their poverty made them subservient to the wealthy ruling aristocracy. Exploiting the labour of the populace, the upper classes created courts of great splendour and subsidized any wars that arose.

The winds of change were blowing, however, brought about by the Enlightment, the beginning of a systematic study of the problems of nature, man and society. Today we take these social sciences for granted, but things were very different in the eighteenth century. Then, society was just beginning to break free from the rigid confines of the class-oriented Medieval Period, led by such great thinkers as Machiavelli, Erasmus and Luther. Like Mozart, these men believed they were making history. Indeed, they had the intellectual gall to name their own "golden age": in Italian—*illuminati*; in French—*lumière*; in German—*Äufklarung*; and in English, the Enlightenment.

The rapid changes associated with the Enlightenment, including those enacted by Emperor Joseph II from Vienna, brought about the emergence of a relatively small middle class, the bourgeoisie. Consisting of merchants, artisans and artists—among them musicians—the bourgeoisie included some emancipated Jews.

This was a turbulent time, politically and militarily. The Seven Years' War took place during Mozart's early years. Freemasonry flourished during the years he lived in Vienna, and the French Revolution began two years before he died.

The Enlightenment brought about considerable progress in the sciences. Man attempted flight using hot air balloons; there was progress in biology and discoveries in the basic medical sciences of anatomy, physiology and pathology. For the first time, clinical descriptions of conditions such as angina pectoris appeared. Despite these advances, there was little appreciable progress in treating illness and in Europe, life expectancy remained startlingly low—between thirty and thirty-six years of age for men.

An almost unimaginably high infant mortality rate was the main reason for these dismal numbers. In Mozart's family, for example, five of his six siblings died in infancy. For those who survived childhood, the prognosis was good, at least among the bourgeoisie. A majority of composers, for example, survived well beyond fifty and some lived to be eighty or more. Those who died before their fiftieth birthdays, about a quarter of the composers, often succumbed to infectious diseases. The prognosis was very likely not nearly as good among the lower classes.

Doctors tended to espouse the Hippocratic axioms that long life depended on proper sleep, diet, exercise, the use of reason and control of emotions; ideas that still apply today. At the same time, the archaic concepts of the "humoral" mechanisms of disease dating to antiquity still generally prevailed.

For their health needs, people turned not only to physicians, but also to surgeons, who tended to be on a lower rung, socially, than physicians, and who often competed with barbers and bathmasters in performing minor surgical procedures, as well as pulling teeth, cutting hair and performing blood letting. Of course, anaesthetics were unknown, so strong men pinned patients down during surgery. Other "health professionals" included apothecaries, midwives and even executioners, who at times tended the sick, using experience they'd gained when attending those subjected to torture. The advice of wise elders and experienced neighbours was also sought.

Treatments, however, were largely ineffective. Bloodletting, purgatives and emetics, all used frequently on patients by physicians, resulted more often in harm than good. It was fortunate, perhaps, that a large proportion of the population either didn't have access to doctors, or didn't trust them. Voltaire is reputed to have said that doctors poured drugs of which they knew little, to cure diseases of which they knew less, into human beings of whom they knew nothing. Instead, people used folk remedies, some of which were quite effective. The use of foxglove, containing digitalis, for example, was of assistance for swelling associated with heart failure. And the vaccination for smallpox, first championed by Britain's Edward Jenner in 1796, was derived from folk sources.

Poverty and poor nutrition, hygiene and abysmal living conditions undoubtedly contributed to ill health and shortened lifespans. The impact of the prevailing economic and financial factors is difficult to determine, because of a dearth of records and significant variations in the value of a currency across the empire. The currency in the Habsburg Empire was a silver florin or gulden, which was divided into sixty kreuzers, but there were regional differences in the value of the currency. Thus four Viennese guldens were worth 41/2 of their Salzburg counterparts. There were also gold coins such as the ducat, which was worth 41/2 guldens, the French louis d'or, worth 71/2 guldens, and the Prussian friedrich d'or, valued at eight guldens. The majority of the Viennese population probably subsisted on an annual income of less than fifty guldens. Wealthier freemen, who held relatively large parcels of land, enjoyed an average income of 200 to 300 guldens. The salaries of people in the service of the nobility, including musicians, might have fallen in the same range. Musicians were treated in much the same fashion as other servants. However, depending on position and experience, more prominent musicians would have commanded salaries several times higher than was the norm. Lead operatic singers, who were in high demand, had good earnings and at times might clear 1,000 to 4,000 guldens from the proceeds of a single benefit concert. On the high end of the economic scale were the noble families, whose huge incomes could reach several thousand guldens annually.

Music played an important part in the lives of the people. The courts of the royalty and higher nobility employed full orchestras, composers, and at times facilities to stage musical theatre. Though music was predominantly the domain of the nobility and the churches, the emergence of the middle class, with money to spend on entertainment, had resulted in growing audiences for musical performances. Members of the public were also increasingly interested in the purchase of instruments and printed music.

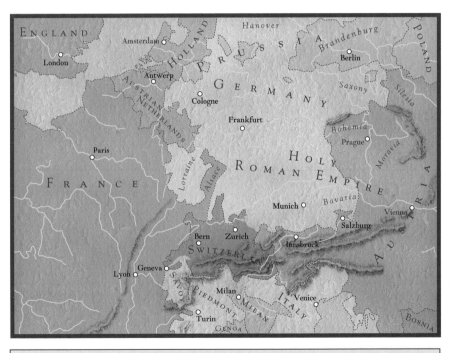

A map of central Europe in Mozart's time

PART I
Mozart

Chapter 1

THE EARLY YEARS IN SALZBURG

The roots of the Mozart family can be traced to the area in and around Augsburg, located in Bavaria in what today is southern Germany. Variously spelled Mozarth, Mozhard, Mozer, Mutzert and Motzhart, the name first appears in parish records in the fourteenth century.

Leopold Mozart, father of the great composer, was born and brought up in Augsburg, where his father was employed as a bookbinder. As the oldest of seven surviving children, Leopold had been studying to become a Catholic priest when his father's death interrupted his studies. Perhaps the disruption caused a change of heart, for soon after his return, he was dismissed for non-attendance. Though he seems to have been a man of faith, he apparently thought poorly of the clergy and decided against entering the priesthood. Instead, he chose a career in music.

Despite his later commitment to his own family, as a young man, Leopold left his widowed mother and younger siblings in Augsburg in order to pursue his career. The rift widened when he married Maria Anna Pertl, for his mother refused him a dowry, something he believed was deeply unfair. Like her, he was prone to grievances and did not accept set-backs easily; the chasm between them was never repaired. When Leopold returned to Augsburg in 1763 with his talented children, his mother, along with most of the city's Catholic community, boycotted the triumphant concerts. The exception was Leopold's younger brother, Franz Alois.

Leopold became a violinist and later Vice-Kapellmeister in the service of Archbishop Schrattenbach of Salzburg. He was a striking man—

in fact he and his wife were at one time considered to be the most handsome couple in Salzburg—and a composer of some ability. In 1756, the same year Wolfgang Mozart was born, Leopold published an important treatise on the technique of playing the violin; sales of the book, as well as teaching, supplemented his modest income from the archbishop.

Methodical and well-educated, Leopold did not marry until he had obtained a salaried position that allowed him to support a wife and family. However, he had an emotional side as well; his classic text on playing the violin not only dealt meticulously with technique, but also emphasized the importance of feeling and emotion in music. And that, he suggested, could be enhanced by studying literature—particularly poetry—which could greatly assist in creating expression.

His only surviving son—Wolfgang Amadeus Mozart—was born in Salzburg at eight o'clock in the evening on January 27, 1756. His father later called him the "miracle which God let be born in Salzburg", likely because of his musical genius, but perhaps also because, though Maria Anna had given birth to seven children, he was one of only two who survived. The other was his sister Maria Anna, named for her mother but nicknamed "Nannerl", born five years earlier in 1751.

The day after his birth, the baby was christened Johannes Chrysostomus Wolfgangus Theophilus. The names were appropriate for a boy who would grow up to be one of the world's great musicians, for Johannes Chrysostomus honoured the feast day of St. John Chrysostom, on January 27th. St. John Chrysostom, Archbishop of Constantinople between 347 and 407 AD, had, in a way, been a musical pioneer who recommended the singing of psalms to enhance the religious experience of worshippers.

The baby was named Wolfgangus for his maternal grandfather, who had experience in music and drama, and Theophilus after his godfather, Johannes Theophilus Pergmayr. Later in life, Mozart preferred the Latin form of Theophilus, which was equivalent to Amadeus (or "God-loving"); it was expressed in French as Amadé, and in German as Gottlieb. Mozart usually signed his mature compositions Wolfgang Amadé Mozart.

The baby seems to have inherited his musical talent from both parents. His mother's family came from the village of St. Gilgen near

Salzburg. Her father had been active in music and drama and that heritage may have contributed to her son's gift for music and theatre, as well as his coarse sense of humour, and fondness for games and jokes.

Tutored by her father, Nannerl had quickly become a talented keyboard player. However, when Wolfgang was just a toddler, Leopold realized that her little brother had astounding musical gifts. He learned to play the keyboard and the violin—the latter without ever having a lesson, according to a family story. He composed his first pieces for the keyboard—short, simple compositions of about twelve measures—before he was five.

Years after the event, a family friend in Salzburg, musician and writer Johann Andreas Schachtner, recalled four-year-old Wolfgang writing "a concerto" in his own notation, filling the page with ink blots, which brought tears to his father's eyes. The work, Leopold said, was too difficult. That is why it is a concerto, responded the child, and needs to be practiced hard. He then sat down at the piano to demonstrate how the piece was intended to sound. Leopold's decision to devote himself completely to the education of his son, and to the presentation of his children to the world, came about after these prodigious talents became apparent.

The early years of childhood are crucial to human development and are greatly influenced by a child's environment and most importantly, his immediate family. Mozart's father, Leopold, was undoubtedly the most important influence on Wolfgang's early development, and that influence continued throughout his formative years.

Leopold's decision to devote himself to developing and promoting his children's remarkable talents was not totally selfless. Though he considered it his duty to God to present his children's wondrous gifts to the world, in the process, of course, he also intended to improve the family's wealth and social standing. He continued in the service of the archbishops of Salzburg until his death in 1787, but his decision essentially put an end to the advancement of his own career as a musician. There are no indications that he was unhappy with this choice, for though he was well-regarded and prolific, he undoubtedly knew he would never be an outstanding composer.

Leopold was promoted to the post of Vice-Kappelmeister in 1763, when Wolfgang was seven. In the years that followed, however, he was passed over repeatedly for promotion to the position of head Kappel-meister, in part because he spent months or even years at a time travelling with his children, but also perhaps because of his difficult personality. His letters reveal a man who was easily dissatisfied and who frequently perceived injustice when events failed to unfold to his liking.

Though he and his family had many friends in Salzburg and made others during their travels, Leopold tended to be suspicious of others. Interestingly, as he grew up, though Wolfgang learned that his father believed people could not be trusted, at times he himself behaved as though he believed the opposite.

Family life in Salzburg was full of social activities, with the emphasis on music making. Visitors who participated in making music included friends in Salzburg and musicians who visited the city, among them those from travelling troupes that came to perform.

Mozart's sister, Nannerl, was studying clavier when Wolfgang was a toddler and beginning to show his outstanding talent. Little Wolfgang wanted to play as well and was soon spending long periods at the clavier, picking out chords and experimenting. Leopold gave Nannerl a music book with simple compositions she was to learn. After Wolfgang began playing, Leopold proudly recorded in Nannerl's book the minuets and other pieces, with the dates and the time it took Wolfgang to learn them. The first of these were before his fifth birthday.

Leopold educated the children with the help of his wife. Each child was assigned work in music and other subjects. As Wolfgang's special talents became evident, their assignments diverged. Among other subjects, young Mozart studied arithmetic, poetry, literature and languages. His sister's education probably emphasized homemaking skills, in addition to music and a general education. Leopold inculcated in his children a trust in God, the idea that their primary duty was to the family, and the necessity for hard work.

Wolfgang's astounding gifts quite rapidly resulted in him becom-ing the person on whom the future of the whole family depended. Leopold believed his talents could be the principal source of the family's income, yet the boy's development continued to amaze him, for Wolfgang took easily to a regime of systematic work. This combination of deep love and high expectations were bound to lead to feelings of heavy responsibility in one so young.

On January 12, 1762, just two weeks prior to Wolfgang's sixth birthday, Leopold set out with his wife and children on the first of many journeys. He had planned carefully, made detailed arrangements, obtained letters of introduction, advertised and sought audiences with royalty and influential members of the aristocracy. This first musical tour took the family to Munich, and a second, the same year, was spent mainly in Vienna. The children performed at the courts of rulers, in the palaces of the aristocracy, and gave public concerts. Their performances, and particularly Wolfgang's, met with great success. The boy performed difficult compositions by sight, sang, improvised and played skillfully on a keyboard that had been covered by a cloth.

At the Imperial Court, the performances were received with great acclaim. Young Wolfgang's abilities were met with amazement and the royal family received the Mozarts warmly, rewarding them with valuable gifts. Elsewhere, the children's performances resulted in cash payments from the aristocracy, and often considerable proceeds from public concerts. Remarkably, during this and subsequent journeys Mozart also wrote a number of musical compositions and some of these early works were published.

After six months back in Salzburg, on June 9, 1763, the family left for a grand journey of more than three years, visiting several cities in southern Germany, as well as Brussels, Paris and London, where they spent more than a year. Returning to the continent, the family went to The Netherlands, Paris again and Switzerland before at last returning to Salzburg. Wherever they went, the children played at the courts of monarchs and aristocrats, and gave public concerts.

During this extensive tour, Wolfgang and his family were exposed to other cultures, languages, art, musical styles and people, including royalty. While all this was of immense educational value, journeys in eighteenth-century Europe were almost inevitably long and arduous. Travelling during the winter and early spring, the family often encountered severe weather and spent long days and nights in uncomfortable, ill-equipped coaches, weeks in inns and accommodation of every description, and endured periods of severe illness. At times, as discussed in Part II, Leopold and the children were confined to their beds for weeks.

As might be expected, young Mozart had a vivid imagination. To pass the long hours when travelling, he created an imaginary kingdom he called *Rücken*—"Back" or "Backwards". The kingdom was enormously detailed, with maps drawn by a family servant. It had subjects and a boy-king, who was of course Wolfgang himself. The name of the kingdom related to Mozart's habit of spelling words backwards. Years later, as an adult, he was known to introduce himself on occasion as "Herr Trazom".

During the months on the road, Wolfgang progressed rapidly as a performer and composer and everywhere met with success and accolades. All this led to growing confidence and a sense of self-importance, which were reinforced by his father.

In London, Wolfgang impressed Johann Christian Bach, one of Johann Sebastian Bach's many children, and played with him. Ever after, the boy held the older master in high esteem. Local newspapers delighted in the children's exploits. In June 1764, an article reported on a concert "for the Benefit of Miss Mozart of Eleven [she was actually thirteen] and Master Mozart of Seven [actually eight] Years of Age, Prodigies of Nature".

Their father, a tireless promoter, explored every opportunity to display the talents of his children and reap the resulting financial rewards. He placed announcements in the *Public Advertiser* that the children would be at home or at a rented hall for two or three hours daily to have their skills tested by the public—for the price of an admission, of course. This dogged pursuit of money and the many public performances he arranged might have adversely affected his standing with the courts, for they may have felt they were not being given due consideration. But it did not seem to affect his relationship with the children themselves.

A glimpse of Wolfgang's public persona and his close relationship with his father can be seen in the following passages, written by Swiss philosopher and educator Auguste Tissot, who saw Mozart in Lausanne in 1766, as quoted by Maynard Solomon in his biography, *Mozart: A Life*:

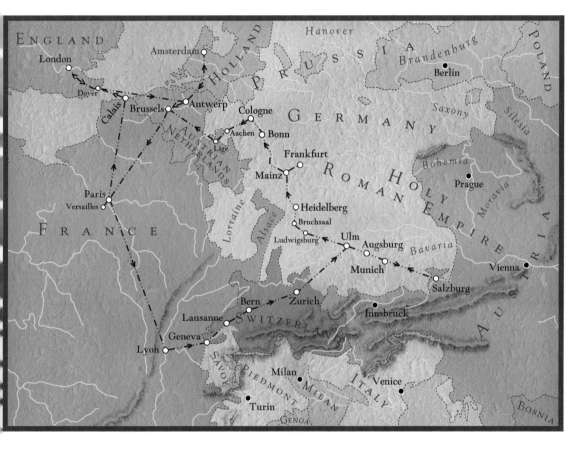

THE MOZART FAMILY'S THREE-YEAR "GRAND JOURNEY" TOOK WOLFGANG, HIS SISTER NANNERL
AND THEIR PARENTS TO FORTY CITIES AND TOWNS ON THE CONTINENT AND IN BRITAIN.
A HALF-DOZEN, INCLUDING PARIS AND MUNICH, WERE VISITED TWICE.

... he has modesty such as is rare at his age, and rare combined with such superiority; it is truly edifying to hear him attribute his talents to the giver of all things and to conclude from this, with a charming candour and in an air of most intimate conviction, that it would be unpardonable to pride himself on them.

Tissot went on to write, "One cannot see without emotion all evidence of [Mozart's] tenderness for a father who seems most worthy of it, who has taken even greater care over the formation of his character than the cultivation of his talents …" He further felt the children seemed "better rewarded by a glance of approval from [Leopold], which they seek with tender anxiety … than by plaudits of a whole audience."

After this marathon journey, the family returned to Salzburg for nine months before leaving again for more than a year. This time, the period away was spent primarily in Vienna, where Wolfgang obtained a commission for an opera, *La finta semplice*, K. 51.

Though he composed it, the opera was not performed in Vienna and though Leopold complained bitterly to the emperor, there was no redress. However, perhaps as compensation for the suppressed opera, Wolfgang was asked to conduct a performance in front of the imperial court at the dedication ceremony of the Waisenhauskirche. This performance included the lost compositions—an offertory, K. 47b, and a trumpet concerto, K. 47c. The opera Wolfgang had written was performed the following May in Salzburg. While in Vienna, Mozart had also composed the operetta *Bastien und Bastienne*, K. 50, which was likely performed at the home of Dr. Anton Mesmer, who is said to have commissioned it.

During the seven years between January 1762 and December 1768, the Mozart family was in Salzburg for only two periods of about nine months each. Though Leopold had taken a leave from his position at the archbishop's court, in addition to the money the children earned with their performances, the family's travels were supported by the Archbishop of Salzburg, who felt that the family's exploits at the royal courts of Europe reflected well on his own court. These trips were likely very expensive, but undoubtedly also resulted in large earnings for the Mozart family.

During these years, the young Mozart composed keyboard pieces, sonatas for violin and keyboard, trio sonatas for keyboard with the accompaniment of violin and cello *ad lib*, early symphonies, some sacred music (for example *Kyrie*), and *pasticcio* piano concertos (K. 37, 39, 40 and 41). The concertos consisted of movements based on solo piano works of other composers, including Carl Philipp Emanuel Bach, to which Mozart added orchestral ritornellos and accompaniments. They were skilfully arranged and used in his concerts. It is also possible that some of the early compositions that were written in Leopold Mozart's hand may have been dictated by Wolfgang before he was able to write music freely. Alternatively, some of these works might represent a collaboration of the son and the father.

After the visit to Vienna, the family returned to Salzburg for about a year. Mozart composed *Missa Brevis* K. 65 in D Minor, *Missa (Dominicus)* K. 66 in C Major for family friend, Cajetan Hagenauer, and serenades K. 63 in G and K. 100 in D, which were likely performed as Finalmusik at the end of the university academic year. In November 1769, young Mozart, then aged thirteen, was appointed Konzertmeister to the court of the archbishop; the appointment was without pay, but the boy received 120 ducats for a trip to Italy.

Between 1769 and 1773, when Mozart was in his early and mid-teens, he and his father travelled extensively. These journeys were intended to present Mozart as a gifted young composer and performer, to seek commissions for operas and to obtain a court appointment. They also offered opportunities to bring in earnings while Mozart could still be billed as a *"wunderkind"*. On December 1, 1769, the boy and his father set out for Italy and stayed more than a year. The trip was filled with positive experiences. However, on occasions when what they expected was not forthcoming, Leopold complained bitterly. Over time, he acquired a reputation of being difficult to deal with, especially by the courts where he was hoping for an appointment for his son. Wolfgang was also growingly sensitive; if his musical prowess was not recognized and readily acknowledged, his displeasure at times led him to react in ways that antagonized influential people and likely interfered with the achievement of his objectives.

This engraving was based on a painting of eight-year-old Wolfgang and thirteen-year-old Nannerl performing with their father in 1864, during the "Grand Journey".

Engraving by Jean Baptist Delafosse, 1764 after Carmontelle
© Internationale Stiftung Mozarteum

Following a break of five months during the spring and summer of 1771, father and son went back to Italy for the four-month autumn season, returning to Salzburg on December 15, 1771. The family spent most of the next year at home, during which time Wolfgang was awarded an annual salary of 150 gulden as Konzertmeister.

In the fall of 1772, Wolfgang went to Milan to stage *Lucio Silla*, K. 135; the opera was performed twenty-six times to large audiences. After this triumphant autumn, and a few months at home, father and son travelled again to Vienna, once more hoping to obtain an appointment for Wolfgang. However, though they were granted a brief audience with Empress Maria Theresa, no appointment was forthcoming and by late September 1773, Leopold and Wolfgang were again home in Salzburg.

Despite their disappointment, these travels, which ended when Mozart was seventeen, were successful in many ways. Father and son made close contacts in the royal courts, as well as with influential nobles and highly placed clergy. They began wearing fine clothing and were at times taken for members of the nobility. Mozart's portrait was painted and he was invited to attend concerts and operatic performances by veteran composers Johann Adolph Hasse and Niccoló Jomelli, among others, which enriched his musical experience. He also gave concerts of his own, composed in various genres and saw many of his compositions performed.

Moreover, Wolfgang obtained high honours; he was admitted to Accademia Filharmonica in Bologna and in Verona after stringent tests. Though, contrary to his father's glowing accounts, he did not do particularly well on the tests, his results were considered "sufficient" because of his youth. Pope Clement XIV awarded him the Order of the Golden Spur and Mozart obtained commissions and composed three operas, which were performed with success.

Mozart's youth and lack of an established track record undoubtedly had some impact on his failure to obtain the appointments he sought. But his lack of success may also have been due to the wide influence of the court in Salzburg; the archbishop and his entourage were obviously aware of Leopold's efforts to leave Salzburg and could have used their connections to thwart them. A letter from the Empress Maria Theresa to her son, Archduke Ferdinand of Milan, advising him not to hire Mozart may have resulted from pressure from the Archbishop of Salzburg. Also, the newly-elected Archbishop Colloredo was not as favourably inclined towards the Mozarts as his predecessor Archbishop Schrattenbach had been, and the archbishop happened to be in Vienna when they had their unsuccessful audience with the empress in 1773.

The many works composed during this period encompassed several genres and made evident Mozart's developing musicianship. The compositions include three operas, more than twenty symphonies (all in major keys); the first mature concerto, for the violin in B flat Major, K. 207; several orchestral divertimentos, including Finalmusik for the end of the academic year at the university in Salzburg; a couple of masses; several short sacred works (among them a concerto-like motet, *Exultate jubilate*, K. 165, for a famous Italian castrato); a half-dozen concert arias for individual singers; a string quartet in G Major, K. 80, and two sets of six string quartets each, all but one in major keys. The two sets show the influence of the quartets, opus 17, by Franz Josef Haydn, with which Mozart was likely familiar.

After returning to Salzburg in September 1773, Mozart spent the next four years at home, apart from a trip to Munich in late 1774. That visit, which lasted four months, was to fulfill a commission for an opera, *La Finta Gardiniera*. Though the opera was successful and Mozart gave concerts, again he was not offered an appointment.

Now in his late teens, Mozart continued to compose extensively and develop his compositional skills and style. He wrote seven symphonies, four violin concertos, five piano concertos, including one for three pianos for Countess Londron and her two daughters, a concerto for bassoon and one for the oboe, a concertone for two violins with solo parts for the oboe and cello, several serenades for patrons and for Finalmusik, compositions for wind ensembles, arias for voice and orchestra, six piano sonatas (composed during the stay in Vienna for the staging of *La Finta Gardiniera*), and church music for the court of the archbishop.

The church music included more than a half-dozen masses and litanies for voices, choir, strings and organ, and early church sonatas. In these works Mozart acquired experience in juxtaposing voices of the soloists and choirs with instrumental support. Among the latter was a remarkable polyphonic offertory, *Misericordias Domini* in D Minor, K. 222. In the symphonies, Mozart experimented with the three-movement Italian model, the Viennese and German type of four movements, and also combined elements of both styles. Among the symphonies, the most notable are probably the "Little G Minor" Symphony, K.183, modeled on Josef Haydn's "Farewell" Symphony no. 45 in F sharp Minor, and the symphony in A, K. 201. The serenades exhibited celebratory melodic content and some included *concertante* movements for solo violin.

Perhaps most important, he began developing his concerto style. This probably stemmed from his experience in juxtaposing solo voice with orchestral elements in the operas, including arias with individual instrumental *obbligato* parts, combined with the melodic character of the serenades. The "concerto for voice", *Exultate jubilate*, written in Italy, and the first concerto for violin of 1773 marked the initial steps in this process. The concerto for bassoon exhibits simple, beautiful themes in the first and second movements that are related. In the second movement, the wind instruments play at times a more independent role, alternating with the soloist and supporting his weaving melodic line. The strings, meanwhile, provide a rhythmic background. These features forecast the prominent role of the *harmonie* band of winds of his many Viennese piano concertos, whereas the rhythmic background in the strings anticipates similar patterns in the other compositions, for example, the slow movement of the piano Concerto no. 21 in C Major, K. 467.

Mozart's unique concerto style, which was to manifest itself so magnificently in Vienna, was evident in the splendid 1777 piano Concerto no. 9 in E flat Major, K. 271. Features introduced in this work included an interpolated minuet in the third movement *rondo*, but not until recently was it known for whom it was composed. In the early twentieth century, French biographers had nicknamed it *"Jeunehomme"*; as a result, for close to 100 years, it was believed it was composed for a mysterious French virtuoso— Mlle Jeunhomme—who visited Salzburg. This was largely because Mozart had written in 1778: "Madame Jenomé is here!" Yet not only the spelling, but the difference in marital status was puzzling. Recently, musicologist Michael Lorenz found that the excellent amateur pianist, Louise Victoire Noverre, was the daughter of French dancing master Jean George Noverre. Mozart had met them earlier in Vienna, where Louise married a wealthy merchant, Joseph Jenamy. He later renewed the acquaintance in Paris in 1778.

Chapter 2

The Fateful Trip to Paris

By 1777, Mozart was increasingly feeling that he must leave Salzburg, where opportunities for development were limited. He petitioned the archbishop for leave and obtained it, but Leopold was dismissed as well. His father's petition to be reinstated was granted, but only on condition that he would not be permitted to accompany his son on a trip the two had planned. Though Wolfgang was now over twenty, Leopold believed that he still needed the steadying hand of a parent, and decided to send his wife in his stead. Mother and son left Salzburg on September 23, 1777, travelling initially to Munich and other southern German centres, though Paris was likely the ultimate destination. It was to be a fateful trip.

The twenty-one-year-old musician left Salzburg full of optimism. Away from his father, he was likely looking forward to asserting his personal independence and perhaps also to the possibility of a romance, for which he'd had little opportunity in Salzburg. His (and his father's) main practical aims were to obtain a court appointment, seek commissions for operas and other works, and perform in concerts. These would help to raise his profile as a composer and performer, as well as generate money to defray the considerable expenses of the long journey, which had to be financed otherwise by the Mozart family assets, administered by Leopold Mozart.

Wolfgang was no longer a child prodigy, though he may have been remembered as such. Having to contend with his reputation as a *"wunderkind"* might actually have been detrimental, for now he was faced with establishing himself as a mature musician performer and composer. Though he was an accomplished clavier player and violinist and composed in many genres, outside Salzburg his name as a composer was not well known. Among his youthful compositions, few are widely known and loved today. In short, his best work was still to come. Nevertheless, to present himself as a composer, he was forced to rely on these youthful compositions and expand his repertoire as he travelled.

Since the number of the compositions he could take was limited by the exigencies of travel, he had to choose carefully. He decided to take the manuscripts of his five violin and several piano concertos, scores of two operas (*Lucio Scilla* and *Il Re Pastore*), the Haffner and Londron serenades, the string quartets K. 80 and K. 174, his piano trio K. 254, a couple of masses and a set of piano variations (K. 185). Thus he seemed intent on presenting himself foremost as a composer of operas and virtuoso concertos, and as an accomplished soloist on the keyboard and the violin.

In Munich, Mozart met with the Elector of Bavaria, but was told there was no vacancy. He gave some concerts, which resulted in ten local sponsors unsuccessfully attempting, through collective patronage, to keep Mozart in the city. On October 11th, he travelled with his mother to Augsburg, where they spent two weeks. Here, Mozart visited piano maker Johann Andreas Stein and was much impressed with his instruments, which he considered superior to those of other makers. He gave several concerts during which, in addition to his symphonies being performed, he played piano Concerto no. 6 in B flat Major, K. 238 and, with a local organist and Stein, the Concerto no. 7 in F Major for three keyboards K. 242, the violin Concerto no. 3 in G Major, K. 216, and improvised and played solo works on the keyboard.

His visit to his father's birthplace was a great success, for his performance was reviewed with gushing praise in the local press and he struck up an intimate relationship with his nineteen-year old cousin, Maria Anna Thekla, whom he called Bäsle, or "little cousin". After he left for Mannheim on October 25th, he wrote her letters that have become famous for their coarse humour, sexual innuendos and bathroom references.

Mozart and his mother spent the next four and a half months

in Mannheim, which possessed one of the finest orchestras in Europe and where German opera was being gradually established. Here, Mozart hoped to obtain a court appointment or a commission for an opera from the Elector of Palatinate, Karl Theodore. He formed friendships with the Konzertmeister Cannabich, the German tenor Anton Raaf and two of the Wendlings a flautist and a violinist, whose wives, both opera singers, later created roles in Mozart's opera *Idomeneo*. Mozart also met the Kapell-meister Holzbauer, and the Weber family. He composed arias "Se al labbro mio non credi", K. 295, for Raaf; "Basta vicesti ...", K. 486a, for Dorothy Wendling, the wife of flautist Johann Baptist Wendling, as well as two songs for his daughter.

Fridolin Weber was a musician and a copyist with a limited income. Mozart soon fell in love with his seventeen-year-old daughter, Aloisia, who was an able, but as yet unpolished singer. Mozart taught her and composed an aria "Alcandro, lo confesso", K. 294, which was designed to show off her vocal prowess. He also willingly gave free piano lessons to Cannabich's fifteen-year-old daughter and composed a sonata in C Major, K. 309, for her. In addition to all these commitments, he gave a series of successful and highly praised concerts.

A Dutch physician and amateur flautist, Ferdinand Dejean, commissioned him to compose concertos and quartets for flute, but Mozart only partly fulfilled the commission, largely because he was so engrossed in his relationship with Aloisia. As a result, he was only paid in part, to the great annoyance of his father. Though the Elector of Palatinate had hinted that Mozart might be commissioned to write a German opera, in the end both the commission and an appointment failed to materialize. While this might have been due in part to the opposition of Vice-Kapellmeister Vogel, who had the confidence of the elector and who would likely have been concerned about competition from Mozart, any chances for an appointment were nullified by the death of the Elector of Bavaria on December 30th. The Elector of Palatinate succeeded him, and decided to move his court and government from Mannheim to Munich. He thus had other, more immediate matters on his mind than an appointment or commission for a young musician.

Mozart continued to linger in Mannheim, however, not wanting to leave Aloisia Weber. As the weeks passed without the results that Leopold had hoped for, the correspondence between son and father became increasingly strained. Wolfgang wrote from Mannheim on November 8th:

Dearest Papa!

I cannot write in verse, for I am no poet. I cannot arrange the parts of speech with such art as to produce effects of light and shade, for I am no painter. Even by signs and gestures I cannot express my thought s and feelings, for I am no dancer. But I can do so by means of sounds, for I am a musician. So tomorrow at Cannabich's I shall play on the clavier a whole congratulatory composition in honour of your name day and of your birthday. All I can do today is to wish you, mon très cher Père, from the bottom of my heart what I wish you every day, both morning and evening; health, long life and good spirits. I hope too that you have now less cause for annoyance than when I was in Salzburg ... I now must conclude with a musical congratulation. I wish you as many years of life as years will be needed until nothing new can be produced in music. Now farewell. I beg you most humbly to go on loving me just a little and in the meantime to put up with these poor congratulations until I get new drawers made in my small and narrow brain-box, into which I can put that wisdom which I intend yet to acquire. I kiss Papa's hands 1000 times and remain until death, mon très cher Père, your most obedient son ...

Wolfgang Amadé Mozart

Leopold responded on November 17th:

My dear son, if you are happy, then I am too and your mother, and your sister and all of us. And you must be so, I trust, if you rely, as I do, on God's grace and your own sensible behaviour. ... It is enough if with your common sense you contribute your quota to your own happiness. I for my part shall never cease to care for the welfare of my children, teach them what I can and, as I have done hitherto, use all my efforts on their behalf until I die.

Your old faithful husband and father
Mozart

However, Wolfgang's financial situation was increasingly precarious and on November 20th and 24th, his father, concerned about the expenditures, wrote about his financial burden:

It is quite certain that the journey and the first period of your stay in Paris will necessitate a well-filled purse. You know that we owe Herr Bullinger three hundred gulden and Herr Weiser more than a hundred. I forget how much we owe Kershbaumer, but it probably amounts to forty gulden. In the New Year, I shall be getting bills from dressmaker and tailor, not to mention other trifling accounts of a few gulden and our daily unavoidable expenses. Food does not cost much, but there are other expenses, especially now in the winter, what with wood, candles and many other small items, so that I have to rack my brains to fit them all in. Nevertheless I am willing, if you really wish to go to Paris, to arrange for you to draw there an advance of twenty or thirty louis d'or in the hope that this sum will come back to me doubled or trebled.

Four days later, he added:

You ought to have asked Herr Herzog or somebody in the firm ... to arrange for you to have a small credit elsewhere, as I used to do ... In my letter of 20th I enumerated our chief debts and even so forgot to mention a [rather large sum we owe] to Hagenauer ... So, if Herr Schmaltz had obliged you, I should have been saddled with a bill, *without having received the slightest warning from you beforehand, and that too at a time when it was the last thing I expected.* Very nice of you indeed!

In February 1778, growingly frustrated, Leopold again exerted pressure on his son, reproaching him bitterly and clearly stating that the welfare of the family depended on Wolfgang:

As you know, [I am now in debt to the extent] of 700 gulden and haven't the faintest idea how I am going to support myself, Mamma and your sister on my monthly salary; So it must be as clear as noonday to you that the future of your old parents and of your good sister who loves you with all her heart, is entirely in your hands.
Think of me as you saw me when you left us, standing beside the carriage in a state of utter wretchedness. Ill as I was, I had been packing for you until two o'clock in the morning; I was at the carriage again at six o'clock, seeing to everything for you. Hurt me now, if you can be so cruel!

Urged thus by his exasperated father, who was clearly beginning to doubt his son's capacity to meet life's responsibilities, Mozart reluctantly set out to try his luck in Paris. During his stay in Mannheim, his chief compositions were three flute quartets and a flute concerto for Dejean, two clavier sonatas, four violin sonatas and three arias.

With his mother, Mozart left Mannheim on March 14, 1778, and arrived in Paris nine days later. Initially encouraged, he worked hard composing for the director of the Concert Spirituel, Joseph Le Gros, and teaching the daughters of several aristocrats. He had to contend with composing at the home of Baron Grimm, a friend of the family with whom they had stayed during their grand journey years before, because the apartment that he and his mother had rented was too small to accommodate a clavier. Grimm now tried to help Mozart establish himself in the French capital. Mozart's compositions included two symphonies (one unfortunately lost), music for the ballet *Les Petits Riens*, a *sinfonia concertante* for four wind instruments for his musician friends from Mannheim, also lost, and a concerto for flute and harp, K. 299, in C Major, for the flautist Comte de Guines and his harpist daughter, who was one of Mozart's pupils.

Busy with composing and teaching, Mozart spent most days away from the apartment. As a result, his mother was often home alone and bored, as she had often been during earlier phases of their journey. Since they were forced to be frugal, the apartments they rented were sometimes not heated. In Paris, she had fewer friends and found life more difficult than she had in Germany. On June 19th, she fell ill with a headache, fever and diarrhea. Reluctant at first to be seen by a doctor who was not German, she delayed seeking treatment. Her condition deteriorated and she died on July 3rd.

Mozart was distraught, but after her death was thoughtful enough to write to his father that his mother was gravely ill, in order to prepare him for the inevitable. He feared that the sudden news of her demise might cause a fatal reaction in his father. At the same time, he wrote to a family friend in Salzburg telling him the truth and asking that he break the news, gently, to Leopold and Nannerl. Mozart then followed with details of what had actually happened in his next letter, trying to convey strength to his father and sister, while struggling with his own emotions over his mother's death and the difficulties with his musical endeavours.

Not surprisingly, perhaps, his father blamed him for the events that led to his mother's death and wrote on August 27th, "If your mother had returned home from Mannheim, she would not have died." Yet it was Leopold and Maria Anna who had decided that Mozart should not travel alone to Paris and it was Leopold who had pushed Wolfgang to continue on to Paris.

Musically, Mozart's prospects were limited, for he lacked the experience necessary to deal with the realities of the artistic landscape. The attentions of Paris's artistic community were mainly on the return of philosopher and writer François-Marie Arouet—Voltaire—just months before his death, as well as on 'the Bouffons' War' between the factions of Gluck's reforms of French music and Piccini's Italian music. Though Mozart was apparently offered a post as an organist to the royal court at Versailles, neither he nor his father was inclined to accept. However, the offer did allow Leopold, by mentioning it, to extract from the Archbishop of Salzburg the promise of an appointment for Wolfgang as a court organist, with a decent salary.

Lingering in Paris, Mozart composed the piano sonata K. 310, in A Minor, one of only two in a minor key of his eighteen works in this genre. The modulations and character of the themes might well reflect his grief following his mother's death. This might also be the case in the sonata for violin and piano, K. 304, in E Minor, which though begun in Mannheim, was completed in Paris. The latter was one of a set of six (K. 301 – K. 306), which Mozart dedicated to Maria Elisabeth, Electress of Palatinate.

Though Mozart came to thoroughly dislike Paris, he delayed leaving, perhaps unwilling to admit that he failed to achieve his goals and to face the likelihood of returning to Salzburg to resume service to the archbishop and the role of obedient son. His procrastination led to acrimonious disagreements with his sponsor, Baron Grimm, who had to contend with his by-now troublesome visitor, who borrowed funds that he had no realistic prospects of repaying. Finally, Grimm insisted that Mozart leave. Rather than go straight home, the young musician went for a few days to St. Germain, where he spent time with Johann Christian Bach, who had come from England. This visit with a man Mozart considered a master and a leading composer of concertos was likely a welcome respite and their discussions might well have been useful in Mozart's future development of the concerto form.

Mozart finally left Paris for good on September 26th, travelling to Mannheim through Nancy and Strasbourg. During his two-week stay in Strasbourg, he gave three poorly attended concerts. Though his father urged him to go to Munich, Mozart instead went to Mannheim, arriving on November 6th. He was anxious to see Aloisia Weber, with whom he was still in love, but alas, her family had moved to Munich, their financial fortunes greatly improved. Aloisia had been engaged by the Munich court opera, with a large annual salary of 1,000 gulden, and her father was also gainfully employed. Disappointed, Mozart lingered in Mannheim, where he enjoyed the musical climate and company of friends. Though the elector's court had moved to Munich, he naively continued to hope for commissions or an appointment.

Assessing the circumstances, his father now exerted tremendous pressure to induce his son to travel to Munich and then on to Salzburg, where the appointment at the court of the archbishop awaited. The pressure included a threat to send letters to his supporters outlining debts of more than 800 gulden that he had undertaken to finance Wolfgang's travels. "In short," he wrote on November 19, 1778, "I am absolutely determined not to remain covered with disgrace and deep in debt on your account; and still less to leave your poor sister destitute."

Mozart left Mannheim on December 9th and arrived in Munich on Christmas Day, but was devastated to find that Aloisia, who was establishing herself as a rising singer, had lost interest in him. Despite that, he stayed with her family. Three days after Christmas, Leopold wrote again. "I have told you repeatedly that our interests and my prospects demand that you should return to Salzburg."

On January 7, 1779, Mozart presented the Electress Maria Elisabeth with his violin sonatas K. 301 – K. 306. But he continued to delay his return to Salzburg, reluctant to again become archbishop's courtier and worse, to return without accomplishing his journey's goals. Perhaps to gain an ally with whom he could return home, he wrote to his cousin Bäsle, asking her to come and join him in Munich. The day after presenting his sonatas to the electress, he wrote to his father that he would like his cousin, who had meanwhile arrived in Munich, to come with him to Salzburg to visit the Mozart family. Though Leopold was somewhat reluctant, Wolfgang and Bäsle travelled to Salzburg, arriving at last on January 15th.

From Mozart's perspective, the journey must have seemed a dismal failure. He had lost his mother, failed to obtain an appointment or even make enough money to pay his expenses, and Aloisia Weber had rejected his affections. Viewed from the twenty-first century, however, it is clear the trip had redeeming factors. Mozart had come in contact with musical styles

This unfinished painting of Mozart by his brother-in-law Joseph Lange is, according to his widow Constanze, the one that was most like him.

Unfinished oil on canvas by Joseph Lange, about 1789 © Internationale Stiftung Mozarteum

in Mannheim, Paris and other cities, absorbed them, and further developed his compositional skills. He had gained experience in dealing with local courts, patrons, musicians and instrument makers and made himself and his talent known to them; all this would serve him well later in his career. He had also survived bitter disappointments and an unrelenting barrage of disapproving letters from his father. And he had developed a loving relationship with his cousin. Though he may not have realized it at the time, these experiences had enriched and matured him, better equipping him to deal with the vicissitudes of life that were yet to come.

Bäsle remained with the Mozarts in Salzburg through the spring, leaving in April. She seems to have been more experienced than Mozart and he might have been concerned about venereal disease, as Mozart had met the composer Josef Myslivecek, the "father of Czech opera", who was disfigured by treatment for syphilis (and eventually died of the disease). Bäsle and Wolfgang were unlikely to have had much opportunity for intimacy in Salzburg; but perhaps in the end he could not bring himself to resist his father's objections—Leopold had made allusions to her "favours" for priests— or he may have been reluctant to consider marrying such a close relative.

Mozart accepted the position of organist to the court of Archbishop Colloredo, whom he disliked, with an annual salary of 400 gulden. In his correspondence prior to returning, however, he had insisted on certain conditions. These included participation in the court music primarily as a keyboard player rather than as a violinist and, perhaps more important, that he would be granted permission to travel to advance his musical career. Leopold wrote to his son prior to his return to report that his demands would be met.

Wolfgang carried out his duties in the months that followed, composing masses, vespers, psalms and church sonatas. The masses, particularly the K. 317 and K. 337, both in C, showed further development of his musicianship. Mozart himself apparently thought highly of them;

years later, in 1791, he had their manuscripts in Vienna and intended to perform one of the masses at St. Stephen's Cathedral. The *Vesperae sollennes de confessore*, in C Major, K. 339, probably the last composition for the court in Salzburg, was a magnificent setting of psalms and *magnificat* for vocal quartet, choir, winds, strings and timpani. He also composed three symphonies, K. 318 in G Major, K. 319 in B flat Major and K. 338 in C Major. The G Major work, with a Turkish theme, was probably intended to be the overture to a singspiel, *Zaide*, which was never finished; it was found among Mozart's papers after his death.

Other works from this period included the "Posthorn" Serenade in D Major, K. 320, the Concerto no. 10 in E flat Major for two pianos, K. 365, presumably for performance with his sister, and the *Sinfonia Concertante* K. 364 in E flat for violin and viola. The last of these shows the evolving freedom of Mozart's compositional style with its prominent and imaginative treatment of the exchange of motifs and developmental material between the soloists.

During this time, Mozart seems to have further matured while living with his father. Perhaps he found him less threatening in person than he had the often bitter and venomous man of the letters Wolfgang had received during his difficult trip to Paris. In any event, father and son appear to have resumed their close relationship. However, Wolfgang also realized that his musicianship had developed to a high level during his travels and he became determined to become independent and seek opportunities to showcase his talents outside Salzburg. Having tasted independence, he likely intended to regain it at the first opportunity.

Leopold, too, was more at ease, with two salaries coming into the house, but he could not see a bright future for himself and his daughter in Salzburg either. Having been repeatedly turned down, he felt he was unlikely to be promoted to the position of Kappelmeister and he was concerned with Nannerl's fate, for unless she married, she had limited prospects. Thus he was hoping that his son's prodigious talents would lead Wolfgang to settle elsewhere, and then assist his father and sister in joining him.

There were differences, however, in how father and son envisaged Wolfgang's future in terms of the best way to earn a living. Leopold felt strongly that a salary related to an appointment was essential, because it provided a steady source of income including exigencies associated with potential illness. While the advantages of such a situation were clear to him, he did not seem to take into account the difficulties in obtaining an appropriate position, though neither he nor Wolfgang had been successful despite their extensive contacts and travels. Nevertheless, he continued to cling to the hope that his son's successes would secure him a position.

Wolfgang probably looked at things differently. He'd begun to earn money from freelance work during his trip of 1777–1778, and had also discovered that, under the right conditions, a group of patrons might pay him to provide compositions on an ongoing basis. As pointed out by biographer Ruth Halliwell, the seed of that notion might have been planted while he was still in Salzburg. There, Wolfgang had often composed music that was not related to his court duties, but rather for friends and patrons. Among them was the influential Countess Lützow. There is also a letter that suggests that a Count Czernin was going to pay Wolfgang 100 gulden a year for compositions. Though the count died soon afterward, and there is no evidence that Mozart was ever paid, he remembered the idea and referred to it in a letter to his father from Munich on December 19, 1780.

In the summer of 1780, Mozart had received a commission for an opera from the Elector Karl Theodore in Munich. This was probably the result of the seed he planted with the elector during his visit to Mannheim. Mozart began composing the opera in Salzburg, working with the librettist Abbate Giambista Varesco, a chaplain at the archbishop's court. Obtaining permission for a leave until December 18th, in order to stage the opera, he left for Munich on November 5, 1780. Except for a visit three years later, he was not to return to Salzburg.

Though the city had been Mozart's official residence for the first twenty-five years of his life, during this lengthy period, he spent almost as much time away from Salzburg as he did at home. Between leaving on his first trip, in January 1762, when he was just five years old, until his final departure in November 1780—a total of nineteen years—Wolfgang was away travelling for more than ten years and in the city of his birth for approximately nine.

Mozart continued to work on the opera after arriving in Munich. It was an *opera seria*, *Idomeneo, rè di Creta*, K. 366, based on the events in Crete after the Trojan War. Introducing modifications to the traditional style, he integrated many arias into the action by having them emerge from a *recitative* and then, without interruption, follow with another *recitative*. Mozart also utilized accompanied *recitatives* more extensively than had previously been the custom. He worked feverishly, stimulated by the presence of the excellent orchestra, which had moved with the elector from Mannheim to Munich and was directed by his friend, Kappelmeister Cannabich.

Letters flew between Mozart and his father, who had begun to serve as conduit between his son and the librettist Varesco. In this way, Mozart requested and obtained many alterations to the libretto as the composition proceeded. Young as he was, he had a keen dramatic sense that led him to demand that parts of the libretto be scaled down. He was also interested in accommodating both the wishes and the limitations of the singers. For example, Mozart modified the arias for his friend, the aging tenor Raaf. However, he refused to make changes, especially to the ensembles, which would compromise musical integrity. An example was the quartet in Act III, "Andrò ramingo, e solo" (I shall wander forth alone), in which Idamante, the son of the king of Crete, faces exile. Mozart sang this quartet with his family when he visited Salzburg in 1783. As related many years later by his widow, Mozart burst into tears while singing it. Perhaps this deep emotion was a result of his identification with the story told in the quartet, for he had left his own family after composing *Idomeneo* and despite mutual visits, may have felt in a sense exiled.

Yet Leopold and Wolfgang worked well together as the composition proceeded, with Leopold doing his best to get Varesco, who was growingly exasperated, to continue to make changes, and prepare the libretto for printing both in Italian and in a German translation. Mozart also needed to obtain mutes for wind instruments, which were not available in Munich. Leopold sent the mutes and made some useful comments about the composition.

December 18th, the official end of the leave for which the archbishop had given consent, passed, but the rehearsals continued. The musicians and the elector were impressed with the work. Mozart's father and sister arrived to hear the opera on January 26, 1781. The next day, which was Mozart's 25th birthday, the dress rehearsal was held and the première took place on January 29th. The opera was a great success. In fact, *Idomeneo* was probably the greatest *opera seria* of the eighteenth century and repeated performances were staged during the next month. It then disappeared from the repertoire and was not staged again during Mozart's lifetime, except for a private concert performance in 1786.

Mozart enjoyed the success and lingered in Munich. He composed the aria "Misera, dove son!" K. 369, for Countess Paumgarten, a mistress of the elector, and the oboe quartet in F, K. 370, for the principal oboist Friedrich Ramm. With his father and sister, he visited Augsburg, where he and Nannerl played music for two keyboards. Nearly thirty years after Mozart's death, his widow related to visitors Vincent and Mary Novello that Mozart had considered his time in Munich to be the happiest period of his life.

There was another reason why Mozart lingered in Munich; he was still hoping to obtain an appointment with the elector. Yet once again this did not materialize. The electress would have been at best indifferent to his engagement, in view of his favours for her husband's mistress, and Archbishop Colloredo, who could have been forgiven for being increasingly upset with Mozart's prolonged leave without permission, might have warned the court that Mozart was simply not reliable. The young composer's absence was particularly noticeable since the archbishop had moved his court temporarily to Vienna to be with his father, who was ill, and was entertaining there without his clavier player. He finally ordered Wolfgang to join him.

Leaving his father and sister behind, Mozart left for Vienna, arriving on March 16, 1781. After the success of his opera in Munich, he was looking forward to exploring his opportunities in the capital and was probably determined, consciously or subconsciously, to settle in Vienna and to become independent of both the Archbishop of Salzburg and his father.

Chapter 3

Blossoming in Vienna

As soon as he arrived, Mozart began giving a series of successful concerts for the archbishop, as well as at the residences of the nobility. Within the first three weeks, he composed the *rondo* for horn, winds and strings in E flat, K. 371, a *rondo* for violin in C, K. 373, for the violinist Brunetti, and the violin sonata in G, K. 379, for himself and Brunetti. The latter was composed near midnight for performance the next day in front of the archbishop and Emperor Joseph II. Lacking the time to write out the keyboard part, Mozart played it entirely from memory.

It was soon clear that his talents were being well received in Viennese aristocratic circles. Now, at last, he felt he could find success as an independent performer and composer, though he continued to hope for a court appointment. Tormented over cutting his ties with Salzburg and facing the objections of his father, he was nonetheless determined to become independent and, perhaps, to be married. To accomplish this, he needed to free himself from the service of the Archbishop of Salzburg and establish himself as an important player in the musical tapestry of Vienna.

Mozart had been unhappy with his lot as a member of the archbishop's court. In part, this was due to the archbishop's refusal to allow him to give concerts for his own benefit, but Mozart was also upset because he was obliged to share quarters with the archbishop's entourage, to live with the cooks and servants and take his meals with them. He was expected to be present every morning at his master's apartments, but did not attend him unless directly summoned. The situation came to a head when the archbishop started to move his staff back to Salzburg, for Mozart did not want to return. He struggled with not wanting to jeopardize his father's position with the archbishop and with the guilt evoked by his father's remonstrations. Leopold was drawing Wolfgang's salary in Salzburg, ostensibly to assist with liquidating the debts that Leopold had incurred to finance Wolfgang's trip to Paris.

In his correspondence with his father, Mozart did not hide his deep dislike for the archbishop. The correspondence was censored, and initially the Mozarts used a code when writing to one another. Then, exasperated, Wolfgang abandoned the code. The archbishop was enraged, but the young musician refused to be cowed. In a letter that showed little respect for his employer, he asked to be released from service and was told to clear his things from the quarters of the court.

After packing up his belongings, Mozart moved to a rooming house operated by his old friend Frau Weber, whose husband had died soon after they had moved to Vienna. But Mozart was not quite free yet. His father continued to reproach him, relying on bits of information he gleaned from others about his son. And the archbishop delayed Mozart's release while a Count Arco tried to mediate. Mozart was determined however, and this persistent intransigence eventually resulted in him literally being kicked out by the count on June 6, 1781. Understandably upset at his treatment, Mozart defended himself in his letters to his father. He could not compromise his honour, he said, by returning to Salzburg and serving at the court. What went unsaid was that he could not bear being again under the influence of his father when he could see so many opportunities for himself in Vienna.

Meanwhile, life in Mrs. Weber's rooming house was much to his liking. The facilities were comfortable and the flexible meal times convenient, given his busy schedule. And then there was nineteen-year-old Constanze Weber, with her pleasant manner and pleasing singing voice. She seemed to soothe the ache her sister Aloisia had created when she rejected him in Munich and the companionship quickly grew into romance. Though Mozart was in fact eager to get married, initially he denied it in his letters to his father, who feared that a relationship with Constanze would loosen his hold on Wolfgang. Frau Weber, on the other hand, was much in favour of a marriage between the two. She likely felt that Mozart had good prospects, and undoubtedly had heard rumours that a commission for an opera or perhaps even a court appointment was in the offing. Adding fuel to the fire, she began circulating rumours of her own about the young couple.

Frau Weber was not to be trifled with. The previous October, she had forced the artist Joseph Lange, who had been courting Aloisia, to marry her after she became pregnant. To quell the talk that he and Constanze were about to be married, Mozart moved out of the rooming house in August, but Frau Weber was not dissuaded; soon she had forced Mozart to sign a contract of intent to marry Constanze within three years. Should he fail, the contract stipulated that he would pay an annual sum of 300 gulden. Constanze, who wanted no part of this coercive behaviour, tore up the contract. The situation rapidly deteriorated, with Frau Weber making Mozart's visits unpleasant, and Constanze moving out to the home of Mozart's patron, Baroness von Waldstätten.

Frau Weber was having none of that and, according to a letter from Mozart to the baroness, threatened to have the police bring Constanze back home. To end this ridiculous drama, Mozart felt obliged to marry Constanze quickly and wrote to his father, asking his permission. Not surprisingly perhaps, Leopold balked and fired off a series of acrimonious letters. But believing that they had no alternative, Wolfgang and Constanze were married on August 4, 1782 at St. Stephen's Cathedral. Leopold's grudging permission arrived by mail, after the fact.

Leopold felt strongly that a young man should not marry without having a steady income. Leopold himself had not married until he had steady employment. He was also aware that by marrying, Wolfgang would be obliged to take care of his own family; the hope that his son would care for him in his old age and provide for his as-yet-unmarried sister faded. In Leopold's eyes, Wolfgang had not fulfilled his filial duties. Yet Leopold himself had left his widowed mother, never to see her again.

Despite promising to send money to his father from Vienna, it's unlikely that Wolfgang ever contributed to the support of his father and sister, largely because he had to take care of his own family. The familial pattern of fracture between Leopold and his mother replayed itself in the strain between Leopold and his son.

Despite the underlying difficulties with his father, marriage greatly settled Mozart's home life, and he began exploring various avenues to promote his musical talents. Concert performances seemed the best way to earn money, gain exposure to potential patrons and members of the court, and obtain paying pupils from among the patrons and other music lovers. Performing his own works allowed him to display his talents as a serious composer, which would lead to commissions for operas, and to sales of his compositions for publication. Thanks to his musical genius, all this came about with little difficulty. His performances were soon the toast of Emperor Joseph II and the aristocracy. During concerts, he improvised on the clavier and played his piano concertos to great acclaim.

He was soon sought after as a piano virtuoso and influential families, many with connections to the imperial court, began to offer support. Entertaining in the salons of patrons and friends, he was eagerly received and highly praised. This was Mozart in his element. Since childhood, he had loved to play the keyboard, entertaining admirers—sometimes even without monetary rewards, much to the dismay of his father. Now he was paid for at least some of his private performances, invited for meals at the homes of noble families, and able to choose eager and capable pupils.

Among his most important early patrons were Countess Maria Wilhelmine Thun, who was considered one of the most cultivated ladies in Vienna; Count Johann Philipp Cobenzl, an imperial vice-chancellor, who invited Mozart to spend time at his summer retreat; Baroness von Waldstätten, who had helped Mozart and Constanze through the difficult time leading up to their marriage; Baron Gottfried van Swieten, the prefect of the Imperial Library, who was himself a musician and had Mozart arrange J.S. Bach's and Handel's music for regular performances at his residence; the publisher, Johann Thomas Von Trattner, who would become godfather to four of Mozart's children, and Court Councillor Franz Sales von Greiner, at whose salon writers and artists gathered. Mozart gave lessons gratis to von Greiner's daughter Caroline, who became, as an adult, a pianist and a writer.

Finally free and independent, Mozart easily acquired four

valuable pupils: Countess Thun; Countess Rumbeke, who was related
to the Cobezl family; Madame von Trattner, and Josepha Auernhammer.
Mozart stayed for some time at the home of Josepha's parents after he
moved from Frau Weber's and may have received the lodgings and board
for an adjustment to his fees for their daughter's lessons. Josepha, who was
described by Mozart as fat and ugly, fell in love with Wolfgang, pursuing him
until he was forced to frankly rebuff her advances. However, he did appreciate her musical ability and her progress on the clavier and dedicated six
violin sonatas to her: K. 296, composed in Mannheim and K. 376 – K. 380,
the last four of which he composed during the spring and summer of 1781.
Artaria published the set of sonatas in December, as Opus 2. He probably
also composed the sonata in D for two pianos, K. 448, for Josepha to play
with him. They performed it, as well as Concerto no. 10 for two pianos
in E flat, K. 365, during a concert held at the Auernhammers' home on
November 23, 1781, which was attended by the members of the Viennese
nobility.

Mozart charged fees of six ducats a month for lessons, not
inexpensive for the time, and his earnings from teaching were equivalent to
800 gulden over the eight months between the autumn of 1781 and the late
spring of 1782, when the Viennese nobility left the city to summer in the
country. This was approximately twice the annual salary he'd drawn in
Salzburg. Undoubtedly a significant proportion of these earnings were spent
on fine clothing, which he felt he needed in order to fit into Viennese high
society and teach and perform in the residences of his patrons. On a typical
day, he was wakened at six by his hairdresser, finished dressing by seven,
composed until ten, and then gave lessons to his pupils three times a week.

But Mozart was still primarily a composer and he was always
looking for commissions. In an effort to gain a commission for an opera,
Mozart played the music from *Idomeneo* to show his abilities in this genre.
But the Viennese public was not interested in *opera seria*. The royal court
was another potentially promising arena for commissions, but Mozart had
to wait his turn, for other composers, including Christoph Willibald Gluck,
who were employed by the court, had priority. And as always, he continued
to hope for a court appointment.

Unfortunately, the emperor favored Italian musicians, a number of whom had his confidence and were concerned about competition from a talented newcomer. Mozart may also have been considered too outspoken for court etiquette. Nor would the emperor have been unaware of Mozart's spat with the archbishop, as well as the latter's views of Mozart, and he may have remembered Leopold Mozart's bitter complaints when Wolfgang's opera *La finta semplice* was not staged in Vienna in 1768. As a result, the emperor chose to use Mozart's talents on an *ad hoc* basis, which also had the advantage of being less expensive for the court.

Mozart had obtained a commission for an opera in July 1781. It was a singspiel, *Eintführung aus dem Serail* (K. 384), the libretto of which contained both humour and human drama. Mozart felt that the Viennese public would appreciate it. The plot was similar to that of his unfinished singspiel *Zaide* (K. 344).

He now started composing with enthusiasm. The story had a Turkish setting and a character named Konstanze. Mozart corresponded and discussed details of the opera with his father, who made various suggestions for alterations. However, Wolfgang was confident of his musical ideas and stood his ground. He cooperated well with the librettist Stephanie and suggested specific changes to the story that fit well with his overall plan. The music, masterfully composed, was used to bolster the unfolding plot. Mozart tailored it to the vocal attributes of the singers and to the emotions and characters of the personalities in the story.

Though he was making good progress, by autumn he realized that the opera would not be performed any time soon, because the court wished to perform the music of the ailing and venerated Gluck.

Mozart had no choice but to be patient. He taught, participated in concerts and entertained in the salons of the Viennese nobility and bourgeoisie. He fit well into the social fabric of Viennese high society and witnessed events, intrigues and personalities that likely provided him with models for some of the characters in his later operas.

An opportunity for close contact with the emperor presented itself during the visit to Vienna of the Russian Grand Duke Paul and his wife. As part of the entertainment for the visitors, the emperor arranged for a keyboard contest between Mozart and virtuoso pianist Muzio Clementi on Christmas Eve 1781. The emperor declared Mozart the winner because of his musicality and sent him fifty ducats, a sum that corresponded to half his annual salary in Salzburg. Mozart also hoped to obtain a commission to compose music for a wind band, or *harmonie*, which the emperor had engaged to entertain him during his meals. To demonstrate what he could do, he composed the wind serenade in E flat, K. 375. The serenade rapidly became popular and, he wrote in a letter, he was himself serenaded with it the following summer in the courtyard of his apartment on his name day, July 27th. He did not get the commission from the court, however, perhaps because his work was more complex than the simple tunes the emperor liked.

Mozart also composed two serenades for wind ensemble K. 361, and K. 388, probably with other potential patrons, who were forming similar *harmonies*, in mind. Though they were beautifully crafted, Mozart did not get the hoped-for commissions. He was later to use the transcription of the music of the serenade K. 388 in his string quintet in C Minor, K. 406.

In March 1782, Mozart gave his Lent concert, during which he played the piano Concerto no. 5 in D Major, K.175, music from *Idomeneo* and improvised. A concert in the Auergarten in May included one of his symphonies and Concerto no. 10 for two pianos, K. 365. On November 3rd, he took part in a concert by Josepha Auernhammer.

Meanwhile he continued to work on the *Eintführung aus dem Serail*. His music expressed superbly the emotions: the rage of Osmin, the overseer of the harem, and the bravura aria of Konstanze in which she grows in maturity and stature and challenges Pasha Selim. Her strength spurs on her intended, Belmont, forecasting the spirit of the aria of Pamina in *Die Zauberflöte*, while the benevolent act of the Pasha seems to portend similar acts of forgiveness in Mozart's future operas. Mozart might have seen his bride-to-be in the character of Konstanze and perhaps Pasha's act as the forgiveness and blessing he was seeking from Leopold. The opera was first performed on July 16, 1782 and quickly became a great success. It was performed in several European cities, including Salzburg, to high praise and on August 6, 1782, two days after Mozart was married, was performed at the request of Gluck, who showered Wolfgang with praise and invited him to dinner.

In spite of these accolades, there were no letters of congratulation from Mozart's father. Smarting from his son's marriage and the realization that the young composer no longer needed his musical input, Leopold continued to reproach Wolfgang. Relying on malicious claims and rumours, he accused Wolfgang of offending the musicians of Vienna and of being lazy. Mozart was a child no longer, however; he stood his ground and after a time the correspondence took on a more amiable tone.

Mozart sent his father scores of his compositions and informed him of what was happening, while Leopold responded by sending Wolfgang compositions he requested. Prior to his marriage, Leopold had requested his son to compose a symphony to honour the ennoblement of a family friend, Siegmund Haffner, in Salzburg. Despite a heavy load of composing, teaching and performing, Wolfgang worked on it, creating a composition in Leopold's favourite key of D Major, K. 385, perhaps to induce his father to accept his marriage and grant his blessing.

The successful première of the *Eintführung aus dem Serail*, K. 384, and Mozart's marriage established him in Vienna. His friends referred to the *Eintführung aus dem Serail* as the *Eintführung aus dem Auge Gottes* (i.e.: the abduction of Constanze from the home of her mother). Though Wolfgang wanted to bring Constanze to visit his father and sister in Salzburg soon after the marriage, the visit was postponed a number of times. Constanze soon became pregnant and with the roads in poor condition because of the inclement fall weather, travel was considered hazardous for her. In a letter home in mid-October, Mozart admitted that he had also delayed because of opportunities that arose with the new season that was beginning with the return of the nobility after the summer break. He was also hesitant to go to Salzburg because he feared reprisals by the archbishop. In a letter to his father in May 1783, he suggested that they might be better meeting in Munich.

Prior to that, Mozart performed in a concert given by his sister-in-law, Aloisia Lange on March 11, 1783 and gave his own academy concert two weeks later. The program of the latter was ambitious. Mozart played his piano Concerto no. 5 in D, K. 175, with the recently composed *rondo*, K. 382, as replacement for the original third movement. The *rondo* with its boisterous flare—in the Mannheim style—became his most popular composition to date. He also played his piano Concerto no. 13 in C, K. 415, a short solo fugue to oblige the musical tastes of the emperor, who was in attendance, and sets of variations on one aria by Paisiello (K. 398) and another by Gluck (K. 455). The variations not only paid tribute to these well-known composers, but also displayed Mozart's musicianship.

The program included Aloisia Lange and two other singers performing arias from Mozart's operas *Lucio Silla* and *Idomeneo* and two concert arias, K. 369 and K. 416; two concertante movements from the "Posthorn" Serenade in D, K. 320 and the "Haffner" Symphony in D, K. 385. His concert was a tremendous success and the highlight of the musical season. The emperor sent Mozart twenty-five ducats, as a mark of his favour.

Mozart continued to explore all the avenues to present his musical prowess and to benefit from it; in May, he wrote that those avenues included the possbility of composing another opera. In a letter to Leopold, he wrote that that the Italian *opera buffa* was starting again and mentioned that a poet, Lorenzo da Ponte, recently appointed as court librettist, might be able to write a libretto for him after fulfilling other obligations. This was not a certainty, however, for da Ponte had been ordered by the court to provide a libretto for Salieri, the court composer and conductor of the Italian opera since 1774 who was to become the Imperial Kappelmeister in 1788. Therefore, Mozart asked his father to determine whether Varesco might be available in Salzburg to provide him with a libretto.

But Mozart was also weighing other options. Despite the high regard in which he was held by many patrons, the emperor had made no effort to keep Mozart in Vienna. Perhaps Paris would offer better possibilities, he reported to his father, adding that he had written to the director Joseph Le Gros to enquire about possibilities for engagements for Concert Spirituel and Concert des Amateurs. Needing quick cash, he wrote to J. G. Sieber in Paris, offering to sell three piano concertos and six string quartets that he was composing, but the offer was not taken up.

Originally Mozart had offered the first three Viennese piano concertos (no. 11, K. 413, in F; no. 12, K. 414, in A; and no. 13, K. 415 in

C) composed during the latter part of 1782 and early 1783 as a subscription. These could be played with just a string quartet, with the wind instruments being *ad lib*. He described the concertos in a letter to his father as:

> a happy medium between what is too easy and too difficult: they are very brilliant, pleasing to the ear, and natural, without being vapid. There are passages here and there from which the connoisseurs alone can derive satisfaction; but these passages are written in such a way that the less learned cannot fail to be pleased, though without knowing why.

However, he was not getting many subscribers and therefore apparently borrowed money to have them published. The enterprise led to difficulties, even though Artaria eventually published the concertos and his string quartets. Both the subscription series and the attempt to sell his work resulted from Mozart's ongoing money problems. Though he was becoming an acclaimed musician and composer, and was earning what should have been a good living, in February 1783 he had written to Baroness von Waldstädten asking her to bail him out. A loan had been called in earlier than expected. In truth, Mozart had developed a pattern of borrowing to pay off previous debts. His financial problems stemmed not only from what might be seen as necessary expenses of living among the upper classes, but seem to also indicate that Mozart was living beyond his means in other ways—attending and giving balls, for example, apparently unconcerned with the consequences. He probably felt that his income would sooner or later allow him to right his affairs.

Mozart did work very hard, composing in several genres. His output during this brief period included the three new piano concertos; two *rondos* to replace previous movements of piano concertos; the first concerto for French horn, K. 417, and a quintet for the horn and strings, K. 407, both in E flat, for his friend Joseph Leutgeb; serenades for winds; three string quartets, K. 387 in G, K. 421 in D Minor and K. 428 in E flat; a flute quartet in C Major, K. Anh. 171; a set of sonatas for piano and violin; piano variations and fantasias, and vocal cannons.

Mozart was also continuing to develop his compositional gifts, in part as a result of his exposure to the fugues of Bach and Handel through his association with Baron van Swieten, who championed their music. Intrigued and determined, Mozart set out to learn the art of fugal composition, intending to modify fugal style and polyphonic counterpoint and incorporate them into his music. He began collecting scores of fugues of Johann Sebastian Bach and other composers, and asked Leopold to send others from Salzburg. The result of his participation in the musical meetings at the baron's residence included arrangements of J. S. Bach's fugues for string trio (K. 404a) and another set for string quartet (K. 405).

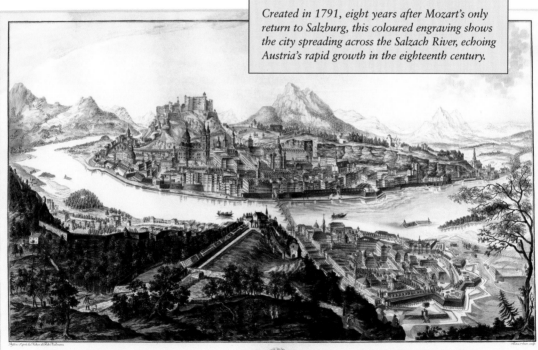

Created in 1791, eight years after Mozart's only return to Salzburg, this coloured engraving shows the city spreading across the Salzach River, echoing Austria's rapid growth in the eighteenth century.

VUE DE LA VILLE CAPITALE DE SALZBOURG AVEC LA FORTERESSE.

Dédié à l'Illustre Chapitre de l'Eglise Metropolitaine de Salzbourg.

Constanze came to like fugues very much and regularly asked
for them. For her, he composed the fugue in C Major, K. 394. And later, it
seems that Mozart and his wife played a more sophisticated composition in
C Minor, K. 426, for two pianos. Nevertheless, these were not compositions
that even Mozart was able to toss off before breakfast. His study of fugal
techniques and counterpoint and his attempts to incorporate them into his
style were clearly laborious, as evidenced by the sketches and exercises for
keyboard left as unfinished segments. Examples include fugues K.deest in
E Minor and K. 401 in G Minor, and a Handelian suite in C Major, K. 399.

This period, which has been called Mozart's "Bach crisis", occurred
when he was composing piano concertos and string quartets, the latter to
be dedicated later to Josef Haydn. He had also begun an elaborate mass in C
Minor, K. 427, which contained fugal passages. The mass was undertaken
to fulfill a vow made prior to his marriage, when Constanze was indisposed.
The mass was to be performed during the couple's intended visit to Salzburg.

On June 17, 1783, Constanze gave birth to their first child,
Raimund Leopold. Mother and son came through the birth with no problems and near the end of July, with the baby doing well, Wolfgang and
Constanze left the infant in Vienna with a nurse and set out on the short
journey to Salzburg. They had intended to stay for a few weeks, but the
visit dragged on until nearly the end of October, likely because Mozart
needed more time to compose the unfinished parts of the mass, prepare the
scores and rehearse. He also worked with Varesco, the librettist, on the
opera *L'oca del Cairo* ("The Cairo Goose"). And of course, there were the
long overdue visits with family and friends.

An account of Mozart's activities in Salzburg, as documented by
his sister in her diary, refers to social events, excursions and music making
with family and friends. Leopold and Nannerl received Constanze politely
but coolly, making it clear that they did not think her a worthy member of
the family. The archbishop ignored Mozart, and the mass was performed at
the monastery of St. Peter rather than at the archbishop's cathedral. Still, the
archbishop turned a blind eye as musicians from his orchestra participated in
the rehearsals and the performance. He must have realized that their services
were needed to perform the richly scored work.

While in Salzburg, Mozart also composed elaborate piano sonatas (K. 330 in C, K. 331 in A, and K. 332 in F), which he would use in future concerts and for teaching and publication. He also composed two duos for violin and viola, K. 423 in G and K. 424 in B flat, to aid his ailing colleague, Michael Haydn. Haydn's indisposition had prevented him from completing a set of six such duos that the archbishop had commissioned, so Mozart obliged. Though he was careful to emulate Haydn's style, the music is remarkable, including double-stopping at times, which gives the impression of more then two instruments. Mozart had not finished the mass, but it was nevertheless performed on October 26, 1783, with Constanze singing one of the solo soprano parts. The day after the performance, Mozart left Salzburg, never to return.

The return trip took Mozart and Constanze through Linz where, at the invitation of Count Thun, they stayed until almost the end of November. The stay must have been pleasant and profitable, for Mozart seemed unconcerned about keeping his pupils waiting for him in Vienna. As a sign of his gratitude, he composed a grand symphony in C, K. 425, nicknamed "Linz", apparently in five days (though he may have achieved this fantastic feat by using previously sketched ideas or notes). While in Linz, he also composed the piano sonata K. 333 in B flat, a brilliant work containing a written out cadenza, likely intended for his own concerts.

The couple finally returned to Vienna on November 30th. It is not clear whether they had learned of their infant son's death earlier, in Salzburg, but now, back in Vienna, they mourned him. The infant death rate in the late eighteenth century varied significantly, but was in some places astoundingly high by today's standards. In Paris, for example, the *survival* rate of foundlings ranged between just twenty and forty per cent; in other words, between sixty and eighty per cent of orphans died. In Mozart's own family, only two of seven siblings had survived the first two years, but in Leopold's father's family, seven of nine survived.

Their mourning ended, Wolfgang's life resumed. On December 22nd, he was asked to participate in the charity concert of the Viennese Society of Musicians during which he played a piano concerto. At last, he was on a course that was to take him to the heights of popularity in Vienna and beyond.

Chapter 4

TRIUMPHS AND TRIBULATIONS

During his first three years in Vienna Mozart had established himself as a première composer and piano virtuoso. This he achieved by giving concerts, primarily during the seasons of Advent and Lent in the late winter, in the residences of the aristocracy or rich bourgeoisie. Now Mozart was ready to reap rewards on a larger scale. Concerts took place at the residences of Prince Johann Baptist Esterházy and Prince Galitzin, the Russian ambassador, who became Mozart's ardent patrons—joining Baron van Swieten and others. Mozart also entered into an association with the impresario Philipp Jakob Martin to stage a series of concerts in Augarten, the public park and, during good weather, in city squares. He planned a subscription series at Trattnerhof, a private hall, with pianist Georg Richter, and invited colleagues and advanced pupils to share the stage with him. During Lent, when the resident companies did not use the imperial theatres, Mozart conducted and performed his compositions in the formal venues such as the Burgtheater. By arranging these series of concerts, Mozart was instrumental in elevating the musical life of Vienna to a level comparable to that of Paris.

Through the 1784 and 1785 seasons, the program of performances was incredibly ambitious; between late February and the end of April 1784, Mozart gave or participated in more than twenty concerts. Though he used previously composed and popular piano concertos and orchestral compositions, this flurry of performances demanded new material and he threw himself into composing with great fervour.

On February 9th, he began keeping a thematic catalogue of his works; the first entry on that date was the piano Concerto no. 14 in E flat Major, K. 449. Three more piano concertos—no.15 in B flat, K.450, no. 16 in D, K. 451, and no. 17 in G, K. 453, were finished by April 10th. Though at least one concerto might have been begun earlier, this was nonetheless a tremendous feat, for it was achieved while Mozart continued to teach and perform. He wrote to his father, "Pupils consume my entire morning, almost every evening I perform" and "of necessity I must play new things".

Barbara Ployer, daughter of the court councillor, Gottfried Ignaz von Ployer, was his star pupil. "Babette", as Mozart called her, participated in Mozart's concerts, often playing compositions created just for her, including the concertos in E flat and in G. In June, she played the latter at a concert at her family's country home in the village of Döbling. The concert also included the sonata for two pianos, K. 448, which she played with Mozart, as well as a recently composed quintet for four winds and piano in E flat, K. 452, with Mozart at the keyboard. Mozart considered the quintet to be his best composition at the time.

For the 1785 season, he composed four more concertos between September 1784 and March 1785. They included no. 18 in B flat, K. 456, composed for the blind virtuoso Maria Theresia Paradis, no. 19 in F, K. 459, no. 20 in D Minor, K. 466, and no. 21 in C, K. 467. The last concerto of 1785 was no. 22 in E flat, K. 482, composed on December 16th and likely performed on December 23rd during a performance of Dittersdorf's *Esther* at the Burgtheater. This is the first piano concerto in which Mozart uses a pair of clarinets, in this case, replacing oboes. The third movement *rondo* includes an interpolated minuet, an innovation that Mozart previously had used in his forward-looking Concerto no. 9, K. 271 in E flat, which was composed in Salzburg eight years earlier, in 1777.

These concertos demonstrate a further stage in Mozart's evolving style. With the exception of the first in the series, K. 449, which may be performed with the accompaniment of a string quartet, the others require sets of wind instruments. In addition to the basic complement of pairs of oboes, horns and bassoons, the flute makes its appearance in the K. 450

and is used in all piano concertos Mozart composed thereafter. The trumpets and timpani are included in four (nos. 16, 19, 20 and 21), though the parts for no. 19 have been lost, and clarinets appear in no. 22. His experience with juxtaposing voices with orchestra and individual instruments in the *obbligato* arias in his operas may have played a part in developing this concerto style. Mozart elevated the role of the wind *harmonie* band, which plays "solo" passages and becomes a full-fledged partner, balancing and providing contrast with the parts of the soloist and the strings. As discussed in detail by musicologist and biographer Konrad Küster, Mozart experiments with tonalities, lengths of the sections, transitions, and parts played by the soloist and the orchestra. In all these respects he went beyond the norm. The result was works of complexity and beauty without equal, at least at the time. The slow middle movements epitomize Mozart's exquisite, weaving melodies, full of emotion and feelings of longing.

At the same time, during the second half of 1784 and 1785, important events were taking place in Mozart's family. In August 1784, Mozart's sister Nannerl married Johann Baptist von Brechtold, an older widower with five children who lived in the village of St. Gilgen, where their mother had been raised. After her marriage, Mozart expressed concern that his father was now living alone and suggested that he either move to live with Nannerl or come to live with him in Vienna.

Nannerl continued to play the piano and was always eager to get her brother's works, despite her relative isolation, limited musical resources and the considerable work she had taken on to care for her new family.

Leopold and his daughter remained very close. Leopold advised her on daily matters and shopped for her regularly. When she gave birth to a boy in July 1785, her father prevailed on her and her husband to let him care for this newborn grandson in Salzburg, offering to bear the cost. Though the baby became seriously ill soon after his birth, he recovered and thereafter helped to fill a void in Leopold's lonely life. Leopold continued to work and took on pupils who lived with him; the most noted were siblings named Marchand. Young Heinrich Marchand would later accompany Leopold to Vienna to play a concert there, which was arranged by Wolfgang.

Mozart continued to be interested in his sister's welfare after her marriage, as evidenced by his letter of August 18, 1784 in which he expressed his concens about his father being left alone. In it, he also included advice on married life in the form of a poem, and suggested that Nannerl, too, might consider moving to Vienna with her family, where she could command better earnings from teaching.

On August 23rd, Wolfgang fell ill while attending a performance of an opera by Paisiello. The illness, which lasted for several weeks, coincided with the late stages of Constanze's pregnancy. Their second son, Carl Thomas, was born on September 21st and a week later the Mozarts moved into a spacious apartment on Domgasse 5. The rent was 450 florins, equivalent to Mozart's annual earnings in Salzburg. The larger space was now needed to run Mozart's household, provide conditions for him to compose intensively and oversee copying of the scores. The copying had to be supervised on the premises, to guard against the high risk that extra copies might be produced by copyists for their own profit. Mozart felt he could now afford the high rent. His earnings from the concerts were considerable and he was offering his compositions, both new ones and some composed in the past, for publication. In 1784 and '85, there were numerous advertisements for his compositions in the newspapers and the resulting sales added to his income. For example, he sold the six quartets dedicated to Haydn to Artaria for the handsome fee of 100 ducats.

In February 1785, Leopold Mozart arrived for a visit. As noted earlier, Leopold had asked Wolfgang to arrange concert appearances in Vienna for the young violinist Heinrich Marchand who, together with his sister, a pianist, were Leopold's pupils and living with him in Salzburg. The Marchand family paid the travel expenses for Leopold and Heinrich to and from Vienna, but Heinrich's concerts were of questionable success. Leopold nevertheless witnessed the beehive of activity at the Domgasse apartment and the hectic schedule of concerts, which he attended. There were about a dozen during his stay, featuring Wolfgang playing four new piano concertos that he had composed between the end of September 1784 and March 1785.

Leopold was not only deeply moved by the beauty of the harmonies and modulations, but also impressed to see his son being saluted by the emperor and heaped with high praise by Josef Haydn following the performance of his string quartets. Yet he could be forgiven for having mixed feelings at the acclaim, for he had tried to dissuade Wolfgang from taking this course and had predicted a disastrous outcome.

It seems that Leopold was also aware that, despite the accolades, the significant income the concerts realized, and the invitations for sumptuous meals in genteel surroundings, his son was still not on a solid financial footing. Perhaps because of this realization, he seemed to appreciate Constanze for her modest and efficient management of the household.

Wolfgang had joined the Freemasons in December 1784 and during his stay in Vienna, Leopold also became a Mason. Though his initiation was accelerated, it nevertheless delayed his departure and in the end, the whirlwind visit lasted two months before Leopold finally left on April 25th. In what seems to have been a real reluctance to see him leave, or perhaps a certain prescience, Wolfgang and Constanze accompanied him to a village outside the city before saying goodbye. They were never to see one another again.

As indicated earlier, on July 27th, Nannerl gave birth to a son, Leopold, in Salzburg. To please her father, she had come from her married home in St. Gilgen for the birth. This was the boy that Leopold convinced Nannerl and her husband to leave with him and his servants in Salzburg. Perhaps he hoped he might groom another musical genius to take the place of his own son.

In Vienna, Mozart continued to compose in genres other than piano concertos. Among these, the string quartets were probably his greatest achievements. The first, in G, K. 387, was dated December 31, 1782, more than nine years after his last quartet, K. 173, in D Minor. Mozart intended to compose a set of six string quartets, but it took him two years to complete. The next two were composed during the summer of 1783, the fourth in November 1784 and the last two in January 1785. The last of these, in

C, K. 465, is dated January 14th. The very next day, all six were performed for Josef Haydn, to whom Mozart dedicated them later in the year. The last three were played again for Haydn at Mozart's home on February 12th, the day after Leopold arrived. That evening, Haydn declared to the proud father:

> Before God and as an honest man I tell you that your son is the greatest composer known to me either in person or by name. He has taste and, what is more, the most profound knowledge of composition.

It was heady praise indeed, for it's likely that Mozart had undertaken the task of composing the quartets as a result of the publication of Haydn's set of six "Russian" Quartets, opus 33, which were heralded as being "composed in an entirely new style". Haydn set out to give all four instruments individual and important roles, a significant departure from the tradition of having the second violin, viola and cello provide backup to the primary function of the first violin. Like many innovations, the composition had been a challenge and among them, Haydn was apparently dissatisfied with certain aspects of his minuets. He used the designation "*scherzo*", but in reality they were simply minuets, which contained musical jokes and were played faster.

Mozart admired Haydn's accomplishments and the two had a high regard for each other. As was his custom, Mozart set out to assimilate Haydn's innovations, modify them and develop the form in his own way. One might even say, particularly in the case of the string quartets, that Haydn and Mozart played a friendly game of "whatever you can do, I can do better". Haydn's earlier set, opus 17, led to Mozart's sets of "Italian" (K. 155 – K. 160) and "Viennese" (K. 168 – K. 173) quartets. Haydn's opus 33 resulted in Mozart's superb "Haydn" quartets and these in turn influenced the older master's later works in the genre.

In *Mozart: A Musical Biography*, Küster analyzes Mozart's innovations in detail and dissects the progress he made as he laboriously composed the set over two years. He notes that Mozart altered the minuets by modifying them rhythmically so that they lost their traditional dance character, apparently building on Haydn's earlier work in the minuets of opus 17. Mozart used fugal techniques in some of the quartets, fusing them with the sonata form, as well as current classical forms. These aspects were already evident in the final movement of the first quartet, K. 387. As he moved through the six works, he imparted weightier roles to the lower instruments. He also employed unexpected suspensions, mutually contradictory passagework and harmonic audacities, the most striking the largo introduction at the beginning of the last work of the set, "The Dissonance", K. 465 in C. These elements were so unusual that some contemporary musicians thought there were printing errors! In September 1785, Mozart dedicated the quartets to Haydn in this moving manner:

To my dear friend Haydn,

A father who had decided to send out his sons into the great world, thought it his duty to entrust them to the protection and guidance of a man who was very celebrated at the time and who, moreover, happened to be his best friend.

In like manner I send my six sons to you, most celebrated and very dear friend. They are, indeed, the fruit of a long and laborious study; but the hope which many friends have given me that this toil will be in some degree rewarded, encourages me and flatters me with the thought that these children may one day prove a consolation to me. Please then receive them kindly and be to them a father, guide and friend. I entreat you, however, to be indulgent to the faults which may have escaped a father's partial eye, and, in spite of them, to continue your generous friendship towards one who so highly appreciates it.

The works truly were the "fruit of a long and laborious" endeavour. Apparently Mozart never found creating string quartets easy, despite his otherwise amazing facility with composition. The surviving manuscripts contain many corrections, changes and erasures.

Mozart joined the Freemasons in December 1784 and over the next six years, he composed and performed a number of works for his Masonic brothers, an indication, perhaps, of the importance the movement had in his life.

Freemasonry appears to have emerged as a result of the development of medieval crafts and guilds, of which the Masons formed one of the most important. Originating in England in the eighteenth century, it spread through much of Western Europe, including France and Austria, as the ideas of the Enlightenment took hold. Masonic societies were secret, with elaborate rituals and rules of initiation. They were dedicated to the consideration and practice of higher things, the meaning of life, the brotherhood of man, and spirituality. The membership included both the nobility and the bourgeoisie, including artists. The liberal reforms of Emperor Joseph II, initiated soon after he ascended to the throne, helped the Freemasons to flourish. However, during the latter part of his reign and under his successor during the last decade of the eighteenth century, regulations were imposed to decrease the number of lodges in Austria as a result of concerns related to social unrest and the French Revolution.

Mozart's Masonic music, apart from the symbolic Masonic content in *Die Zauberflöte*, consisted of several works in 1784 and 1785 and others thereafter, including one that was composed less than a month before his death. Mozart was considered to be one of the most important Masons of the eighteenth century.

Mozart attended about a dozen lodge meetings during the first year after he joined; at these meetings he met a number of influential individuals and formed friendships. These included officials of the Imperial Court and members of several noble families, among them Baron Gottfried von Jacquin, who became a close friend; banker Johann Michael Puchberg, who was to become Mozart's benefactor, and clarinet virtuoso Anton Stadler. These relationships led to social and musical gatherings at the residences of patrons and friends, some of which were attended by the emperor.

A Whirl of Composition

OTHER WORKS THAT MOZART COMPOSED during 1784 and 1785 include: a piano quartet in G Minor, K. 478, composed in October 1785, and intended as the first of a set of three for publication by Franz Hoffmeister. The work was too difficult for amateurs and poor demand led Hoffmeister to ask that the project be aborted, although Mozart completed a second work, which in contrast was bright, in the key of E flat Major, the following year. In the piano quartets, Mozart was breaking a new ground, fusing the part of the piano with three string instruments. His rich experience in the piano concerto form and the newly developed craft of the string quartet resulted in a pair of beautiful and sophisticated works that paved the way for other composers in a new chamber music genre—the piano quartet.

o Twenty-five pieces for three winds, K. Anh. 229 (439b), probably for basset horns, for the Stadler brothers and likely performed at a concert on December 15, 1785.

o Piano sonata K. 457 in C Minor, dedicated to his pupil Therese von Trattner, published and usually performed with piano fantasia K. 475, also in C Minor, composed a few months later.

o Violin sonata in B flat for the violin virtuoso Regina Strinasacchi and performed by her with Mozart on April 29, 1784 in the Kärtnerhor Theatre in the presence of the emperor (with Mozart apparently playing his part from memory since he did not have time to write it out), and violin sonata in E flat, K. 481.

o The oratorio *Davidde penitente*, K. 469, with input from Lorenzo da Ponte in which Mozart, pressed for time, used music from his mass K. 427. Adding two new arias, this was first performed at the concert of the Society of Musicians at the National Court Theatre on March 13, 1785.

o Six songs, including "Die ihr einem neunen Grad", K. 468, likely performed during the ceremony to promote Leopold Mozart to the Second Degree of the Masonic order on April 16, 1785.

o Cantata "Die Mauerfreude" K. 471, performed on April 24, 1785.

o The *Mauerische Trauermusik*, K. 477, considered the greatest of Mozart's Masonic works. Scored for a large group of winds, including oboes, clarinets, basset horns, horns and strings; it was likely performed on more than one occasion during the second half of 1785, the last time apparently in December in connection with the ceremonies marking the recent deaths of two Masonic brothers.

Mozart had always been interested in composing operas and made considerable efforts to show himself as an able operatic composer. He composed arias for Aloisia Lange and tenor Johann Adamberger for insertion into a performance of an Italian opera, *Il curioso indiscreto*, by Pasquale Anfossi in June 1783. These unfortunately resulted in Mozart being accused of trying to show his superiority to the Italian composer; he was forced to refute these charges in print.

Yet buoyed by the success of the *Eintführung aus dem Serail*, Mozart hoped to compose another singspiel. However, the emperor's court decided to start an Italian opera company and Mozart had been approached to compose for it near the end of 1782. As mentioned earlier, he did start work on the opera *L'oca del Cairo*, K. 422, with the librettist Varesco in Salzburg, and had made fair progress, but the work was never completed. A similar fate befell the work *Lo sposo deluso, ossia La Rivalità di tre donne per un solo amante* ("The Deluded Bridegroom, or the Rivalry of Three Women for the Same Lover"), K. 430, the verses for which might have been provided by the librettist da Ponte. Disappointment at not being able to compose a German work and perhaps reservations about the worthiness of the librettos might have contributed to the slow progress and lack of motivation to proceed more effectively. However, Mozart remained keenly interested in composing another opera.

An opportunity finally arose in the latter part of 1785. The emperor was impressed with Paisiello's *opera buffa*, based on the work "The Barber of Seville" by Beaumarchais, and the court was interested in the sequel "The Marriage of Figaro", so Mozart and da Ponte were approached. The work began, basing the opera on the play minus passages that were less than flattering toward the nobility. Da Ponte and Mozart worked well together and by November the libretto was almost ready. Mozart, who had been composing intensely, reported to his father that he was "over neck and head" in composition. At the same time, he continued to teach and prepare for the winter musical season. Then a decision by the court to use an opera by Martin y Soler for the Carnival allowed Mozart more time to refine the music for "Figaro". An additional delay resulted when the emperor commanded Mozart to provide a singspiel for royal entertainment in early 1786.

These operatic opportunities signalled the changes that were to come in Mozart's career; as his first five years in Vienna were drawing to a close, he was popular and in demand, with significant earnings. Yet debts continued to plague him. On November 20, 1785, he wrote to the publisher, Franz Hoffmeister: "I turn to you with my problem and beg you to assist me with some money, which I need most urgently at present."

Chapter 5

THE YEAR OF CHANGE

Seventeen eighty-six marked both a change in Mozart's musical interests and an apparent downturn in his material fortunes. As the year began, he continued to compose intensively. A letter from Leopold to his daughter refers to three concerts, with 120 subscribers, planned by Mozart. In addition, the work on the two operas seemed to awaken his interest in other genres. The table on Page 71 lists chronologically the works Mozart composed in 1786.

In addition to all of these, at about the same time, it seems he composed a number of vocal works and two separate fragments for piano trio, which he did not finish. Together with a later fragment, they were completed after Mozart's death by a friend of the family, Mathias Stadler, and edited as a trio, K. 442.

According to the date on the manuscript, the first composition of 1786 was a *rondo* for piano, initially dedicated to a pupil, Charlotte von Würben. The dedication was later erased. Biographer Robert Gutman has said that Mozart used in it a theme by Johann Christian Bach, which he had previously quoted in the first episode of the *rondo* of the G Minor Piano Quartet, K. 478. In the K. 485 *rondo*, he developed the theme in the manner of Carl Phillip Emmanuel Bach, thus joining and celebrating the individual contributions of the two famous sons of Johann Sebastian Bach, whom he held in high regard. The songs K. 483 and K. 484 for chorus and organ were performed at the initial meeting of an amalgamated Masonic lodge named "New-Crowned Hope". The lodge had been formed as a result of a decree by the emperor who, growingly concerned about threats to the monarchy, had ruled that the Masons must reduce the number of their lodges. Mozart likely composed the works shortly before they were performed.

An event that might have been related to Mozart's involvement with the Masonic movement occurred on February 19th. He attended a masked ball wearing the robes of an Eastern philosopher and, in keeping with his character, distributed sheets with riddles and proverbs, which he had authored himself. The riddles were in the Shakespearean tradition, but referred to as "Excerpts and Fragments of Zoroaster". Robert Gutman suggests that they may reflect Mozart's unresolved relationship with his father, which could have been awakened by the revival of his opera *Idomeneo*. The opera, which was to be performed the following month, revolves around a strong father-son theme. Mozart sent the riddles to his father, who made light of them but had segments reproduced in a Salzburg newspaper.

The creation of the riddles might also have been a statement reaffirming the continued viability of the Masonic movement, which was an important resource for Mozart as a meeting place of like minds and friends. The following examples of the puzzles provide a glimpse into Mozart's personality: "One can have me without seeing me"; "One can wear me without feeling me"; "One can give me without having me"; "It is not for everyone to be modest: it is appropriate only for great men", and "If you are a poor but noble fool—become whatever you can to earn your bread. But if you are a rich, noble fool, become whatever you want: only not a man of understanding, I won't have that."

The singspiel *Der Schauspieldirektor* ("The Impresario") with the libretto by Stephanie, who had provided the libretto for the *Eintführung*, was performed at a banquet given by the emperor on February 7th to entertain his sister Maria Christina and her husband Albert, ruler of the Austrian Lowlands. The entertainment also included Antonio Salieri's *opera buffa Prima la musica e poi la parole*. Mozart was paid fifty ducats and Salieri 100. "The Impresario" consisted of one act of ten scenes and included an impressive overture and four numbers. The plot, which had been suggested by the emperor, was based on a quarrel between two sopranos, with the leads sung by Aloisia Lange and Caterina Cavalieri, who were rivals in real

The Compositions of 1786

K. Number	Composition & Date
485	*Rondo* for piano in D Major, Jan. 10
483	Song with chorus "Zeifliesset heut" in B flat Major, Jan. 14
484	Song with chorus "Ihr unsre neuen Leiter" in G Major, Jan. 14
486	"Der Schauspieldirektor", Feb. 3
488	Piano Concerto no. 23 in A Major, Mar. 2
489	Duet for soprano & tenor for concert performance of *Idomeneo* ("Spiegarti non poss'io"), Mar. 10
490	*Scena* for concert performance of *Idomeneo* ("Non più tutto ascoltai …" and "Non temer, amato bene"), Mar. 10
491	Piano Concerto in C Minor, no. 24, Mar. 24
492	*Le nozze di Figaro*, May 1
493	Quartet for piano and strings in E flat Major, June 3
494	*Rondo* for piano in F Major (in Sonata K. 533), June 10
495	Concerto for French horn in E flat Major, no. 4, June 26
496	Trio for piano, violin & violoncello in G Major, July 8
487	Twelve duos (for two French horns), July 27
497	Piano sonata for four hands in F Major, Aug. 1
498	Trio for piano, clarinet and viola in E flat Major, "Kegelstatt", Aug. 5
499	String quartet in D Major, "Hoffmeister", Aug. 19
500	Twelve piano variations in B flat Major, Sept. 12
501	*Andante* and five variations for piano, four hands, in G Major, Nov. 4
502	Trio for piano, violin & violoncello in B flat Major, Nov. 18
503	Piano Concerto in C Major, no. 25, Dec. 4
504	Symphony No. 38 in D Major, "Prague", Dec. 6
505	*Scena con rondo* "Ch'io mi scordi di te …" for soprano, orchestra & piano *obbligato*, Dec. 26

life. A tenor (Johann Ademberger) tries to serve as a mediator.

The music of the bravura arias for each soprano and two ensembles made the piece a hit with the audience, despite the thin plot. A repeat performance at another reception, plus three theatre performances, all in February, attest to its success.

The splendid Piano Concerto no. 23 in A Major, K. 488, provides some insight into Mozart's composing habits. He seems to have composed part of the first movement in late 1784 or early 1785. He frequently did this, often creating incomplete fragments to be used later. Some he never finished; others were completed by colleagues or students after his death. (Mathias Stadler, completed a number of works, including the piano trio, K. 442, referred to earlier. Other fragments were finished by clarinetist and composer Anton Stadler, while the requiem was completed by Mozart's student, Franz Xaver Süssmayer.) Mozart probably revived a fragment of his piano concerto in December 1785 and completed it shortly before its première in early March at one of his subscription concerts.

He had initially scored the first movement with oboes, but when he returned to the composition, he decided to use clarinets instead, as he did in the piano concerto in E flat Major, K. 482, which was composed in December 1785. About three weeks later, another concerto, no. 24 in C Minor, K. 491, was ready and was likely played by Mozart at a concert on April 7th. In this concerto, he further explored the limits of the genre; the first movement is in three-quarter time, which Mozart had used in only one other concerto, and it is the only such composition with a full complement of winds, including pairs of both oboes and clarinets. It is a disturbing work, only one of two piano concertos that Mozart wrote in a minor key.

On March 13th, in the midst of writing and performing his own concerts and preparing "The Marriage of Figaro", he staged a private performance of his opera *Idomeneo* at the palace of Prince Johann Auersperg. For this, he reworked the lead role of Idamante, which was originally to be sung by a castrato or soprano, for a tenor voice, and composed two splendid new replacement numbers with verses by da Ponte: the scene with the tenor aria, K. 490, with a beautiful violin *obbligato* played by Mozart's friend and excellent amateur violinist Count Augustus Clemens Hatzfeld, and the duet

K. 489. The changes fit seamlessly into the opera, making it clear that despite the changes in his musical style, Mozart had no difficulty slipping into the spirit of a work written six years earlier. Nor was he hampered by the fact that he was simultaneously working on *Le Figaro*.

Le nozze di Figaro, K. 492, altered Mozart's musical direction and elevated his musicianship to yet another level. He infused its music with the experience he acquired in composing the piano concertos and the string quartets. The resulting music was complex, making it difficult for less refined members of the audience to appreciate it at first. Much had been made of the patterns and progression of the tonalities. Küster points out that Mozart uses the music to echo the plot; he keeps delaying the return to the tonic key of D Major as the plans for Figaro's marriage keep running into various obstacles. The patterns woven by the music, thus matching the emotions and actions of the characters and the turns of the plot, resulted in a masterpiece of undeniable beauty. The strong cast of singers and the members of the orchestra burst into shouts of "Bravo!" when an aria was performed during rehearsal.

Even after modifications had been made by da Ponte and Mozart, the plot had social implications, for the servants Figaro and Susanna succeeded in getting married, thus thwarting the count who, in the end, had to eat crow and apologize to the countess. Despite opposition by some court officials and musicians, the opera premiered on May 1st. The effect improved with repeated performances, as the cast became more comfortable with the music and the libretto. Soon, the audiences were insisting that arias and ensembles be repeated. These demands led the emperor to ban repeating numbers, except for solo arias, to avoid performances of an inordinate length.

For all this, though the opera was performed ten times in Vienna during 1786, Mozart was paid only a one-time fee of 450 florins. And though his still popular *Eintführung* was also performed ten times in Vienna that year and played in other cities as well, these repeated performances gave him no additional earnings. After 1786, *Figaro* was replaced by the highly popular new opera *Una casa rara* by Martin y Soler and was not seen in Vienna again until August 1789, while the *Eintführung* continued to be performed in succeeding years in Vienna and other European cities.

Mozart was busy and happy during the winter and spring of 1786, composing the two operas, concertos and other works, performing and teaching. The success of his endeavours, particularly *Figaro*, was enormously gratifying. As the hectic pace slowed, he was able to spend more relaxing time with his friends and turned to composing mainly chamber music. Some works, written for friends or pupils, must have pleased him, for he set himself various challenges. He also knew that the compositions could be performed in future concerts or offered for publication.

His circle of friends included the von Jacquin family. The head of the family was Baron Nicolaus Joseph, a famous botanist and professor at the University of Vienna. The family occupied quarters in the Botanical Gardens, where scholars and artists gathered in a pleasant social atmosphere to engage in erudite discourse and be entertained. Mozart was friendly with both sons of the baron, Johann Franz who, like his father, was a botanist and became a university teacher, and Emilian Gottfried, who was both a pupil of Mozart's and one of his best friends at the time. A younger sister, Franziska, was one of Mozart's favorite piano pupils and had a pleasant singing voice. During a very busy and successful visit to Prague in January 1787, Mozart wrote to Gottfried:

> Today I have at last been so fortunate as to find a moment to enquire after the health of your dear parents and the whole Jacquin family. I hope and trust with all my heart that you are well as we are. I must frankly admit that, although I meet with all possible courtesies and honours here ... I long most ardently to be back in Vienna; and believe me, the chief cause of this homesickness is certainly your family ... [A]nd I kiss your sister's hands a hundred thousand times and urge her to practice hard on her new pianoforte. But this admonition is really unnecessary, for I must confess that I have never yet had a pupil who was so diligent and who showed so much zeal ... Keep me in your precious friendship.

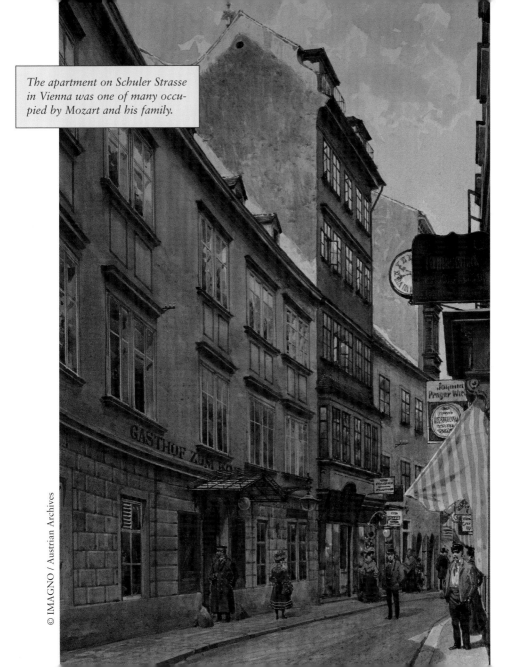

The apartment on Schuler Strasse in Vienna was one of many occupied by Mozart and his family.

Gottfried von Jacquin wrote in Mozart's album:

> Genius without heart is a chimera—for it is not intellect alone,
> not imagination, not even the two combined which make
> genius—love! love! love! is the soul of genius.

It is not surprising therefore that Mozart composed a number
of works for the von Jacquins in 1786 and thereafter. The following year he
composed a double cannon, K. 228, for the older brother and songs for the
younger (some apparently were published under the younger brother's name
with Mozart's agreement, perhaps to assist in his courtships). Regarding
one composition for the family, he wrote from Prague in November 1787:

> If the song en question is to be a test of my friendship, have no
> more doubt on the subject, here it is. But I hope that you do not
> need the song to convince you of my friendship.

According to Caroline Pichler, a daughter of one of Mozart's patrons,
social gatherings with musical entertainment were held regularly at the
von Jacquin residence. She recalled these occasions this way:

> On Wednesday nights, as far back as I can remem-
> ber, social gatherings were held even in winter, when the Jacquin
> family occupied quarters in the Botanical Garden … and when
> in the rooms used by the father, erudite discussions were held
> while we young ones chatted, made music, played innocent little
> games and amused ourselves thoroughly! What a happy, care-
> free period of our youth!

Among other friends were Anton Stadler, a virtuoso on
the clarinet and basset horn, and a group of English artists. That group
included Nancy Storace, an accomplished soprano who created the role of
Susanna in *Figaro*, her brother Stephen, a composer, Michael Kelly, another
member of the *Figaro* cast, and Thomas Attwood, Mozart's valued pupil.

That summer, Constanze was again pregnant and the Botanical Gardens were an attractive place for young families to spend time. The Mozarts had a talented young pupil living with them at the time, eight-year-old Johann Nepomuk Hummel. Apparently Mozart refused payments for the boy's board and lessons.

The first work completed after the première of *Figaro* was the piano quartet in E flat Major, the key of friendship. This bright companion to the darker G Minor quartet, created the previous December, is full of charm and warmth. In this and some of the following works, Mozart draws on his experience with the piano concerto and string quartet forms. All the instruments play important roles and some passages in the piano quartet begin with only the viola and cello playing.

The instrumental set in the piano quartets is that of the piano trio with the addition of a viola. This instrumental complement is only one violin short of the early Viennese piano concertos that Mozart composed with the winds *ad lib*, so that they could be played on the keyboard with a string quartet. However, the character of the piano quartet is different. *Concertante* passages in the keyboard convey to some extent a sense of a "chamber concerto", but the string trio is an equal partner. The piano and the trio take turns playing solo passages and providing accompaniment to each other. Thus Mozart's piano quartets may be considered to be a hybrid of the piano concerto and the piano trio; in short, this was a new genre.

The *rondo* for piano, K. 494, was combined with two movements written two years later to form the piano sonata in F major, K. 533. This was followed by the second concerto for French horn, written for Mozart's friend Joseph Leutgeb and containing a slow, expressive *romanze*. In writing the concerto, Mozart used inks of different colours and this has often been taken to be a joke, meant to confuse Leutgeb; more likely, however, it was a way to indicate the nuances of the intended dynamics. The bright piano trio in G Major followed by about ten years Mozart's only previously composed mature piano trio. That first trio, K. 254 in B flat Major, was in the pattern of a piano sonata with a limited role for the violin and with the cello confined almost exclusively to supporting the bass line of the keyboard. (Though comparatively simple, Mozart had thought this early composition to have taken it with him on his trip to Paris.) In the more mature G Major trio, the string instruments acquire some independence and this trend would evolve even further in the trio in B flat, completed in November, and in the three trios composed in 1788.

Mozart's remarkable ability to create refined compositions while seemingly at play has been celebrated in modern theatre productions and movies such as "Amadeus", but is based on historical evidence. On the manuscript of K. 487, likely a set of duos for horns, Mozart wrote, "July 27 while playing skittles" A few days later, the piano sonata in F Major for four hands was finished. Gutman and Roussel suggest that it was composed for Mozart to play with Franziska von Jacquin at one of the soirées at the Jacquin's residence. Roussel considers it "worthy of inclusion among [Mozart's] masterpieces of chamber music", with the first movement combining the gallant and learned styles, the *andante* in the subdominant—a "noble and solemn piece" resembling "a love-duet from an *opera seria*", and a brilliant *finale* with both mischievous and sensual themes. Mozart wrote another brilliant and difficult keyboard duet in C Major, K. 521, for Franziska the following spring.

The clarinet trio K. 498 is dated August 5, 1786 in Mozart's thematic catalogue. This bright work in E flat Major, which is discussed further in Part III, was followed approximately two weeks later by a dark string quartet, K. 499, composed for his friend and publisher Hoffmeister. The quartet may have been written by Mozart to compensate his friend for the unsuccessful venture of his piano quartets. Albert Einstein wrote of the quartet: "The *adagio* speaks of past sorrow with a heretofore unheard-of depth; and the *finale* is another of those uncanny movements in which the major mode seems to reverse its character—it is not gay, but despairing, or rather it is despairing under a mask of gaiety ..." The bright and dark moods were never very far apart in Mozart's music, whether within the same composition, in works that were paired, for example the two piano quartets, or in compositions that were created close in time, as in the clarinet trio and the string quartet.

It may be only coincidence, but just three days after completing the trio K. 498, Mozart wrote to his family's former valet, Sebastian Winter, who was now in the employ of Prince von Fürstenberg. In his letter, Mozart offered to provide a number of new compositions each year in return for an annual salary. Clearly, he was experiencing ongoing financial strains. While he enjoyed the company of his friends and shared with them his compositions, his economic situation continued to be precarious. Ironically, though his English singer friends were richly remunerated for participating in repeated performances of his operas, Mozart received no benefits from them and he was keenly aware of it. As the summer drew to a close with uncertainties about continued success of his concert series, Mozart felt that his talents were being not sufficiently rewarded in Vienna and he considered seeking opportunities elsewhere.

Mozart's work in preparing for concerts, exploring potential ventures, and family events may explain why only three works, other than some unfinished fragments, appeared over the ensuing two months. They were a set of variations for solo piano, K. 500, another for four hands, K. 501, and the piano trio, K. 502. The variations were likely on Mozart's own themes and little is known about the circumstances of their composition. The exquisite trio continues the spirit of the summer series of the chamber works, with Mozart significantly elevating the importance of both string instruments. This, combined with *concertante* passages for the keyboard, leads to a work that conveys hints of "a concerto in a chamber setting".

On October 18th, Constanze gave birth to a baby boy, who died a month later. For more than a year, Mozart had considered seeking opportunities abroad. His English friends thought he would do well in England. They were planning to return home early in the New Year and Mozart considered travelling with them, accompanied by his wife. Leopold Mozart had become aware of his son's plans during his visit in 1785, and avoided letting him know that he was taking care of Nannerl's child. Mozart learned this from a common acquaintance and in early November —before the death of his infant son—he wrote to ask his father whether he would take care of his children while he and his wife went to England. Leopold indignantly refused. It seems he was eager to care for the son of his loyal daughter, but not the offspring of his rebellious son. In fairness to Leopold, his health was beginning to deteriorate and he was likely concerned about the possibility of having to bring Wolfgang's children to England on his own. He may also have felt that Wolfgang could make other arrangements. But though Mozart's friends tried to set up opportunities for him in England, no firm offer materialized. Without one, it seemed unwise to go.

Leopold's correspondence with his daughter refers to four concerts Mozart was planning during Advent. These were to include two imposing works, the Piano Concerto no. 25, K. 503, and the symphony, K. 504. The piano concerto, in C, is the longest of Mozart's works of this type and a fitting closure to his great period of Viennese concerto writing; over a span of about four years, he had created fifteen such works. Concerto no. 25 is scored with trumpets and timpani, though no clarinets, which Mozart had used in the previous three concertos. And he used material that he had composed almost two years earlier.

According to Albert Einstein, "No other work of Mozart's has such dimensions, and the dimensions correspond to the power of the symphonic construction and the drastic nature of the modulations. In no other concerto does the relation between the soloist and the orchestra vary so constantly and unpredictably." Having met many challenges that he set for himself in the development of the concerto style, Mozart may have lost interest in the genre, for he wrote only two more keyboard concertos, one in 1788 and the other in 1791.

Two days after finishing the piano concerto, Mozart completed the symphony in D, later named "Prague". He composed the *finale*, which formed the third movement of the symphony, in the spring of 1786, perhaps as a replacement for the original final movement of the "Paris" symphony. This and fragments for other symphonic movements at that time indicate his renewed interest in the genre. He seems to have added the first two movements in a rush, perhaps for an imminent performance in one of his Advent concerts. The symphony in D, with its thematic references to the melodies of *Figaro*, would endear Mozart to the audience when the work was performed in Prague. Despite the absence of a minuet, this expansive work, with its new ideas of thematic progression and modulations, and an increased role for the *harmonie* band, is considered a worthy companion to the three great symphonies that Mozart would compose in 1788.

Mozart's music continued to be popular and a number of his works were advertised for sale in newspapers and published throughout the three-year period between 1784 and 1786. Though the precise number of concerts was never documented, an estimate of less than ten in 1786 shows a steep decline, compared to more than twenty in 1784 and between fifteen and twenty in 1785. Was this because Viennese audiences were tiring of Mozart's music, as has been alleged? To whatever extent this might have been the case, it's as likely that other factors were responsible for the decline. First, the extensive work necessitated by the composition and staging of the two operas in 1786 undoubtedly took a lot of time. Throughout his career, Mozart had a keen interest in musical theatre. When he was working on an opera, other genres and activities commanded considerably less of his attention. Also, beginning in 1786, political factors began to play a part in his life, as well as the lives of many others. The economy was in decline and inflation was increasing as Austria became involved in the war against Turkey. The war also meant that Mozart's patrons spent less time in the capital and his audiences had less disposable income for entertainment.

The day after Christmas, Mozart finished the *scena* and *rondo*, K. 505, as a farewell gift for Nancy Storace. Composed for soprano and orchestra, with an *obbligato* piano part for himself, it was to be performed at her final benefit concert in February 1787. Mozart chose to complete it early, because an invitation to travel to Prague had arrived before Christmas. In mid-December, Pasquale Bondini's company had performed *Figaro* in Prague for the first time. The opera's resounding success led to the invitation from the company's orchestra and "distinguished connoisseurs and enthusiasts", who may have been influenced by Count Thun, Mozart's steadfast patron. The invitation asked Mozart to visit soon, perhaps to sustain interest in further performances. And the visit led to a warm and fruitful relationship between the composer and the city, musicians and audiences of Prague.

Chapter 6

The Romance with Prague

Though Mozart's last five years, between 1787 and 1791, have often been considered to be a period of decline, in fact his musicianship continued to progress, and there were indications in the final year of his life that his financial problems might have improved had he not died.

Mozart left Vienna for Prague on January 8th, accompanied by his wife, dog, servant, and four musicians, including Anton Stadler and thirteen-year-old prodigy Maria Cruz, with her aunt along as chaperon. Mozart was always ready to help other musicians, in this case by providing opportunities to perform and gain exposure. They arrived in Prague on the 11th, and Count Thun insisted that Mozart and Constanze stay at his home. On the 12th, Mozart was fêted and entertained, and took part in the music making, likely with his piano quartet in E flat, K. 493. He wrote subsequently to Gottfried von Jacquin that he had been to a "ball where the cream of the beauties of Prague … flew about in sheer delight to the music of my Figaro, arranged for quadrilles and waltzes. For here they talk about nothing but Figaro. Nothing is played, sung or whistled but Figaro. No opera is drawing like Figaro. Nothing, nothing but Figaro. Certainly a great honour for me!"

Five days later, Mozart attended a performance of his opera and on the 19th, by popular demand, gave a concert during which he improvised at the keyboard on an aria from *Figaro* and the symphony in D, K. 504, was performed. Mozart's biographer Franz Xaver Niemetschek was present and provided the following account as quoted by H.C. Robbins Landon:

> The theatre had never been so full as on this occasion ... We did not in fact, know what to admire most, whether the extraordinary compositions or his extraordinary playing; together they made such an overwhelming impression on us that we felt we had been bewitched ... The symphonies he composed for this occasion are real masterpieces ... full of surprising modulations and have a quick, fiery gait, so that the very soul is transported to sublime heights.

On the 22nd, Mozart conducted a performance of *Figaro* to deafening cheers.

Then, early in February, he composed contradanses K. 509 for a music-loving count. There's a story behind this composition; it's said that Mozart had promised to write the dances, but had not done so. The count purportedly invited him for a meal, but when Mozart arrived, insisted that he compose the work before the meal was served. Mozart obliged. It appears that he first wrote the dances in a solo keyboard form and orchestrated them for the count's large orchestra later. Prior to his departure for Vienna, likely on February 8th, he came to an understanding with the company of Bondini to provide them with a new opera for the following season.

Mozart must have been filled with joy at the acclaim he'd received, and according to one of Leopold's letters to Nannerl, he had made a profit of 1,000 gulden from the brief trip.

Back in Vienna, the farewell benefit concert for Nancy Storace took place on February 23rd. It featured the *scena con rondo*, K. 505, which Mozart had written for her with the *obbligato* piano part for himself. Its words, "Ch'io mi scordi dite? / Non temer, amato bene" ("That I will forget you? Do not fear it beloved."), make it clear that this was a heartfelt parting gift for a fine musician and friend. Mozart valued her highly, but apparently without a romantic involvement. Ms. Storace reportedly cleared 4,000 gulden from the concert. Then she, her English friends and their entourage left, travelling through Salzburg, where Leopold welcomed them and Ms. Storace performed for the archbishop.

Back in Vienna, March was a busy time for Mozart, with three Wednesday concerts at the Kärntnertor Theater, including a piano concerto played by the composer, and the performance of his symphonies and arias. Ludwig Fischer, who sang the role of Osmin in *Die Eintführung*, gave a concert on March 3rd, in which he sang the aria "Alcandro, lo confesso …", K. 512.

During the same month, Mozart also composed the aria "Mentre ti lascio", K. 513, for his friend Gottfried von Jacquin, who was a good bass singer, and a *rondo* in A Minor, K. 511, for piano. The unique joyless music of the *rondo* points toward the romantic style of the next century and at times anticipates the style of Chopin. Some twentieth-century musicologists have called the *rondo* the most beautiful work ever composed by Mozart. It was also a composition that Mozart's younger son, himself a professional musician, considered highly. Its somber mood might have been related in some way to the events that were unfolding at the time.

As indicated earlier, Leopold Mozart's health had begun to deteriorate during the previous year; early in 1787 he complained of shortness of breath when climbing stairs and pressure in his chest. He fell ill in early March and his daughter arrived to take care of him in mid-March from the nearby village of St. Gilgen, where she lived.

Shortness of breath and swelling are symptoms commonly associated with heart muscle failure. Such failure may be due to the weakening of the heart as a result of the obstruction of the coronary arteries that supply the heart muscle due to arteriosclerosis, which may lead to angina or a heart attack, or may be due to overwork of the heart, related to narrowed or leaking valves in the heart. The damage to the valves may be the result of previous episodes of rheumatic fever, a complication of streptococcal infection, or to calcification.

Nannerl returned to St. Gilgen in early May to take care of her family, probably assuming her father would be able to manage on his own. Leopold wrote a last letter to her on May 11th, suggesting that although he was weak, his condition appeared to be stable. Then on the 28th, he suddenly died, perhaps alone. Neumayr concluded that his death was due to a myocardial infarction or heart attack. This is a likely diagnosis, with the death resulting from the damage to a large portion of the heart by a further blockage of a coronary artery or a sudden disturbance of the heartbeat, known as arrhythmia.

However, I believe that two items of information raise the possibility of another cause of Leopold's sudden death. First, in his final letter to his daughter, he mentions a pulsation under his stomach. And second, the *Berchtold Family Chronicle*, created by the family of Leopold's son-in-law, states that Leopold Mozart died suddenly at 6 o'clock in the morning of a hardening in the lower abdomen. The pulsation suggests that Leopold may have had an aneurysm of the abdominal aorta, which ruptured, leading to a rapid filling of the abdomen with blood and resulting in abdominal hardening and rapid death.

Wolfgang had apparently heard of his father's ill health and, concerned, wrote to him from Prague, but the letter was lost. He therefore wrote again—his last letter to his father—on April 4th. Ostensibly referring to the recent death of a close friend, amateur violinist Count von Hatzfeld, he writes that death "is the true goal of our existence" and "the key which unlocks the door to our true happiness". He expresses the hope that his father is getting better, but adds if that should not be the case, Leopold should let him know immediately, so he can come to "his father's arms". The letter was never answered and he learned of his father's death from a family friend on May 29th. Mozart himself was ill at the time of his father's death and did not attend the funeral. The disposition of Leopold Mozart's estate is discussed in Chapter 10, Family Finances.

Earlier, during April, seventeen-year-old Ludwig van Beethoven had come to Vienna to study with Mozart. Mozart listened to him play and is said to have predicted that Beethoven would go far. Some lessons may also have taken place, but after just two weeks, Beethoven had to leave because his mother had become very ill.

Toward the end of April, Mozart had moved his family to

suburban lodgings. Not only did the new apartment have a garden, but the rent was considerably less. Though this was always a practical consideration, Mozart's finances seemed to be reasonably good at the time. He had made a handsome profit from his brief visit to Prague and had a commitment to write another opera for Prague later in the year. Though he'd lost a sizable sum when a friend to whom he had loaned funds had absconded without repaying him, about two months later he received 1,000 gulden from his father's estate. A more important reason for the move, therefore, may have been the desire for a quiet location, away from city centre, for his family. Constanze was again pregnant and Wolfgang no longer needed to live in the centre of the city. In the past, when he had been giving frequent subscription concerts, it was important to live near the urban centre. Now, however, quiet surroundings were perfect as he set to work on the new opera for Prague.

Over the succeeding months, the opera progressed slowly, as Mozart explored new challenges by turning to other genres. In April, he completed the string quintet in C Major, K. 515, which was followed in May by another quintet in G Minor, K. 516. As indicated earlier, Mozart had written only one other string quintet, thirteen years earlier. That first composition, K. 174 in B flat Major, had apparently been modelled on a work by Michael Haydn. As had Haydn, Mozart composed his first and the subsequent quintets for two violins, two violas and a cello. However, Küster points out that in his quintets Mozart introduced the use of "two trios": two violins with a viola as the upper group and two violas with the cello as the bass. At times the two trios played simultaneously, with the use of double-stopping by one of the instruments.

The approach that Mozart used in these compositions evolved from his use of the cello as an emancipated voice in the quartets he had dedicated to Haydn. The cello alternates with the first violin or the viola, taking turns at playing the melody. Also, according to Küster, Mozart's advanced experience with the composition of the piano concertos led him to include *concertante* passages that imparted a sense of "a chamber concerto" to these works, with all instruments at times taking the part of a soloist. A similar chamber concerto character can be felt in Mozart's other chamber works of the same period, such as his piano trios. The two quintets of 1787 contain hesitations, suspensions and asymmetries, creating intense emotional tensions. There is an element of grave sadness and even lament, particularly in the G Minor work. Here, a joyless second movement, a minuet, is followed by a poignant adagio. British author Aldous Huxley wrote about the *adagio* in *Antic Hay*: "How pure the passion, how unaffected, clear and without clot or pretension the unhappiness of that slow movement ..."

Remarkably, the last movement begins with yet another grave *adagio* before it gives way to a dance-like *allegro*. If one were to read a personal significance into these string quintets, one might be led to believe that Mozart had composed them and the somber *rondo* in A Minor, K. 511, when he was aware of the failing health of his father, for Leopold had died within two weeks of the completion of the G Minor quintet.

On June 4th, Mozart buried his pet starling, which he had purchased in May 1784. The bird had learned to sing a theme from the *allegretto* of his G Major concerto, K. 453. In his account book, under the entry with the price that he paid for the starling, Mozart had written out the five measures of the bird's song, which was identical, except for the G sharp and the grace notes, with five measures of the *allegretto*. Then he wrote, "Das war schön." ("That was beautiful.") According to an entry in Otto Erich Deutsch's *Mozart: A Documentary Biography*, "When the bird died, Mozart arranged a funeral procession, in which everyone who could sing had to join in, heavily veiled, [it] made a sort of requiem, an epitaph in verse." One can speculate that the elaborate ceremony for a tiny bird was in some way a sublimation of Mozart's grief for the death of his father about a week earlier.

Two weeks after his father's death, Mozart completed *Ein musikalischer Spass*, (A Musical Joke) K. 522, for two horns, two violins, a viola and double bass solo. Some biographers accused Mozart of being heartless, apparently appalled that he could return to work on something that was a 'joke' so quickly, but he had actually begun the composition more than a year earlier and only completed it in 1787. The work contains a number of "incorrect" compositional techniques, modulations and sequences throughout and is often considered a parody of inept composers. Küster, however, feels that only a highly skilled musician could compose such a "perfectly incorrect" work; an analogy would be for a specialist to write an examination in his field with every answer given incorrectly. Interestingly, the third movement *adagio cantabile* contains a cadenza; Mozart had previously incorporated a cadenza in his sonata for piano solo in B flat Major, K. 333.

Though Mozart had lost his father and his close friend, he continued to revel in the friendship of Gottfried von Jacquin and his family. About a year earlier, Mozart had composed a vocal ensemble "Liebes Mandel, wo ist's Bandel?", K. 441, for soprano (Constanze), tenor (Mozart) and bass (Gottfried), with strings. The ensemble originated with a comic episode when Constanze, having misplacing her ribbon, created a frantic commotion in searching for it that involved Gottfried, Mozart and his dog. During 1787, particularly during the spring and summer, Mozart composed more than a dozen other vocal ensembles, canons and songs. Several of these were composed for his friend Gottfried, at times under his name.

Mozart's friendship with Gottfried involved more than just singing, for they enjoyed both serious and frivolous times together. But music was a large part of their relationship and other compositions for the von Jacquin family from that period include a parody flute quartet in A Major, K. 298, and the sonata for four hands in C Major, K. 521, for Franziska.

On August 10th, Mozart entered the serenade *Eine kleine Nachtmusik*, K. 525, in his thematic catalogue. This is one of Mozart's best-known compositions, but Einstein also refers to it as "one of the most enigmatic". Scored for a string quartet and double bass solo, it is more commonly performed by a string orchestra. The "enigma" concerns the occasion that led to its composition; whether it was intended as chamber or orchestral music. Apparently the score indicates "bassi", plural for double bass, but singular "viola", rather than the plural "viole". Whereas Küster feels that it was intended for an orchestra, David Jones, writing in the *Mozart Compendium*, considers that it was likely intended as chamber music. Known now as a four-movement work: *allegro;* romance *(andante); menuetto (allegretto); rondo (allegro)*, it originally included another minuet between the first movement and the romance, which has been lost. The work is beautifully crafted, symmetrical, and generally bright. The romance in C Minor is the only movement that contains some unrest. It is slow, in a *rondo*-like form. As pointed out by Küster, it is structured very much like the romance of the D Minor piano concerto, but contains a *fugato* passage based on a routine cadence that Mozart uses to return to the tonic after the first episode. This little "joke" is the only reminder of the recently composed *Ein musikalischer Spass*. As the title *Nachtmusik* suggests, the work might well have been performed one evening during the summer of 1787. As it came during the period of time when Mozart spent a lot of time, including music making and composition, with and for Gottfried von Jacquin and his family, it might well have been played during one of the Wednesday musical evenings at their residence near the Botanical Gardens. Two weeks after *Nachtmusik*, Mozart completed a violin sonata in A Major, K. 526, which was published later during the year.

Mozart had been asked to compose an opera for Prague during his first trip to that city, undoubtedly to capitalize on his immense popularity. The subject for the work was the legendary womanizer, Don Juan. The story had been previously staged in various forms, most recently in Venice early in 1787. The music for Venice was by Giuseppe Gazzaniga, with a text by Giovanni Bertati. The tenor who sang in the Venice production subsequently went to Prague and it may have been he who suggested mounting the work there. The Bondini Company, having made a commitment to Mozart, thus suggested the topic to him and he accepted.

However opera productions in the Habsburg Empire had to be

approved by the court and had to serve its enterprises. During the summer of 1787, these were complex, for the emperor was making plans for two family weddings, both involving children of his brother, Leopold of Tuscany. The emperor commissioned Salieri to stage an opera in Vienna for the wedding of Prince Francis, and Martin y Soler to compose another for the arrival in Vienna of Archduchess Maria Theresia in October, en route to marry Prince Anton of Saxony. The emperor agreed to approve Mozart's opera for Prague, to coincide with a stop of the princess and her groom in that city, during their journey to the betrothal in Dresden.

Because da Ponte had undertaken the Herculean task of writing the libretti for all three operas, progress must have been slow. Da Ponte's work on *Don Giovanni* was facilitated by the available drafts of previous libretti. Besides Bertati, librettists included Carlo Goldoni in 1736, the great French playwright Jean Baptiste Poquelin—much better known as Molière—in 1665 and Tirso de Molina in 1608. He used this material, but instituted extensive changes with input from Mozart. Even the sequence of some of the events was altered to make the progress more cogent and new material was added to expand the work to two full acts.

Da Ponte and Mozart went beyond the blueprint of "The Marriage of Figaro" in their new opera with the full title *Il dissoluto punito, ossia Il Don Giovanni* (literally, "Punished Libertine, that is, Don Giovanni"). Mozart emphasized the continuity from episode to episode, by including fewer recitatives and solo arias, and using instead more ensembles. There is a pseudo-finale sextet, a first in Mozart's operas, in Act II, when Leporello, Don Giovanni's servant disguised as his master, is caught. The resolution, however, is dissipated. Then follows the graveyard scene. Don Giovanni mockingly invites the statue of the Commendatore, whom he murdered, to supper, and the statue, speaking out, accepts. Here Mozart and da Ponte create a complete change in the character of the work, bringing in a sense of terror and the supernatural. To accomplish this and following the example of Gluck in *Alceste*, which was written almost two decades earlier, Mozart uses trombones in the orchestra.

Mozart's prowess in polyphonic complexities is climaxed in the ballroom scene of the *finale* of Act I, in which three bands on stage simultaneously play three different dances. The first band plays a minuet in 3/4 time for an aristocratic couple, Don Ottavio and Donna Anna; the second joins with a contradanse in 2/4 time for Don Giovanni and the peasant girl Zerlina, and finally the third orchestra plays a rustic *allemande* in 3/8 time for Leporello and Zerlina's peasant lover Masetto. The apparent clash of the three bands underscores the inability of Don Giovanni to smoothly take his exploits across various classes of the society. In the true *finale*, the statue arrives for supper to the sounds of the "Tafelmusik", which in contrast to the clash of the three bands, is orderly. Here Mozart uses music from three other operas in succession: Martin y Soler's *Una cosa rara*, a popular opera with a libretto by da Ponte, which displaced *Figaro* after its initial run in Vienna; Giuseppe Sarti's *Fra i due litiganti il terzo gode* of 1782, and his own hit aria "Non più andrai" from *Le nozze di Figaro*.

The unrepentant Don Giovanni's descent into the underworld is followed by an epilogue in which the remaining characters point to the moral of the story—"the happy ending" of the punishment of Don for his deeds. Entered as *opera buffa* in Mozart's thematic catalogue, it is in reality a *dramma giocosa*. Containing both comic and dramatic human elements, it reaches new heights in the opera genre.

During September, Mozart worked on the opera with da Ponte while mourning the death of another friend, his faithful physician Dr. Sigmund Barisani, who died on September 3rd. The opera was intended to première in Prague in the middle of October, to coincide with the visit of the archduchess and her fiancé. Mozart left Vienna for Prague with his pregnant wife at the beginning of the month and arrived in Prague on the 4th to find that it would be impossible to stage the new opera to coincide with the visit of the princess and her consort. The cast and musicians needed more time to perfect their roles, and some of the singers had fallen ill. (It's also possible that Mozart may have been misled by the cast's polish when he visited early in the year, when they were well acquainted with *Figaro*.)

Instead, permission was sought and obtained to substitute *Figaro*, which was performed for the bridal couple on October 15th. Alternatively, Einstein suggested that Mozart (and perhaps local dignitaries) may have deliberately delayed the new opera, feeling that the story of a libertine was not suitable for the bridal couple, but this seems unlikely, for *Figaro* also contains elements that could offend.

Da Ponte followed Mozart to Prague a few days later to work on the remaining parts of the opera, but had to leave after just a short while at the insistence of Salieri, who demanded that he return to his other commitments in Vienna. The première of *Don Giovanni*, K. 527, took place on October 29th. The initial performance may have suffered as a result of the complexity of the music and the very short rehearsal time. The overture, for example, was apparently played without any rehearsal whatsoever; Mozart supposedly composed it only the night before, with Constanze repeatedly waking him so that he could complete it on time. However the musicians and the cast rapidly mastered the work and it became an unqualified success.

The performance on November 3rd was given for Mozart's benefit. On the same day he finished a concert aria "Bella mia fiamma …", K. 528, for his friend Josepha Duschek. Mozart had spent considerable time on the Duschek's suburban estate during his stay in Prague, perhaps putting finishing touches to the opera. Three days later, Mozart composed two songs: "Des kleinen Friedrichs Geburtstag", using the words that had celebrated the ninth birthday of Crown Prince Friedrich of Anhalt-Desau on December 27, 1778, K. 529, and "Wo bist du, Bild", K. 530, for Gottfried von Jacquin. He sent the latter to his friend from Prague to fulfill a previous promise; the song was apparently published under Gottfried's name. Though Mozart enjoyed his success and was urged to stay in Prague and write another opera, he left on November 13th and was back in Vienna on the 16th.

As Mozart was en route, the venerated Gluck suffered a major stroke and died on the 15th. This event was to have a significant effect on Mozart's situation in the Hapsburg capital. Gluck's death freed 2,000 gulden of his annual stipend from the imperial budget and on December 7th led to the appointment of Mozart as Kammermusicus ("chamber musician") with an annual salary of 800 gulden. Despite Mozart's detractors at the court, the emperor favored him and appreciated his music. Mozart's long-standing supporter at the court was Prince Kaunitz, who once remarked to the Archduke Maximilian that people like Mozart "come into the world but once a century and must not be driven from Germany, particularly when one is fortunate enough to have them in the capital." The archduke probably repeated these flattering remarks to Mozart.

Prince Kaunitz had also been a staunch supporter of Gluck, who was born in Bavaria but attained his greatest exploits and fame in Paris, before settling in Vienna at an advanced age. Kaunitz was likely instrumental in securing the court's generous support, and perhaps in convincing Gluck to spend his latter years in the Austrian capital.

Mozart, however, had hoped for a larger salary. Though the emperor was not known for excessive largesse, it must also be remembered that Gluck was much older and more famous than Mozart when he was given his significantly larger salary. Moreover, a salary of 800 gulden was considered high among courtiers and Mozart's duties at court were limited to composing dance music for the balls at the Redoutensaal. This imposing building, which contained two large halls, was used for staging concerts, balls and other festive events.

Clearly, Mozart hoped that his stipend would increase over time, and the emperor might well have considered this. Mozart remarked that the amount was "too much for what I do, not enough for what I could do". But he proudly informed his sister that he had finally obtained the court appointment that had eluded him for so long. The steady income was helpful, his light duties left him freedom to pursue other ventures, and he might not have appreciated fulfilling the heavy commitments of a fulltime court Kappelmeister.

As 1787 drew to a close, Mozart moved his household from the suburbs back to the city centre, likely because he now needed to be close to the court and perhaps because of other activities in which he was going to be engaged. These included further work for Baron van Swieten, as well as preparing for the production of *Don Giovanni* in Vienna, at the behest of the emperor. His last composition of the year was the children's song "Die kleine Spinnerin", K. 531. On December 27th, Constanze gave birth to their fourth child, a girl, Theresia, who was to live for only six months.

Chapter 7

New Realities

Though the court appointment and the successful trip to Prague were undoubtedly both gratifying and remunerative, Mozart's economic situation continued to be precarious. Not only was the salary from the court insufficient to cover the needs of his family, but he was experiencing a steep decline in the demand for his concert performances, with a resulting loss of income. As indicated in an earlier chapter, this was mainly because of the expensive and largely unsuccessful war against Turkey, which had convinced the nobility to desert the capital, where conditions were deteriorating. As a result, Mozart found himself in much the same situation as he had when he first arrived in Vienna, and now, as then, he was forced to look for other ways to earn income. These included writing and publishing compositions in a variety of genres, composing and staging operas as opportunities presented themselves, conducting and participating in concerts and other musical events, teaching, and pursuing opportunities abroad.

As Kammermusicus, he fulfilled his obligations to the court by composing music for the balls. Between January 1788 and March 1791 he produced eighteen contredanses, fifty German dances and eighteen minuets. These were skilfully crafted and he had no difficulty maintaining his position with the court or his personal standing with the emperor.

Mozart let it be known that he was once again available for teaching, which he had abandoned when his days had become filled with frequent concerts and the time-consuming work of composing for them. He also set to work creating new compositions; the first of these in 1788 was a piano sonata in F Major, K. 533, consisting of two movements to which Mozart added an expanded *rondo*, first composed in 1786 (K. 494). Between June 1788 and July 1789, three further piano sonatas followed (in C, K. 545; in B flat, K. 570, and in D, K. 576). Mozart likely used these works in his teaching. An *adagio*, K. 540, the only piano composition by Mozart in the unique key of B Minor, was composed in March 1788. In February, he completed the piano concerto in D Major, K. 537, which was probably started earlier, though he may not have played it until his journey to Germany the following year.

Early in 1788, he also arranged his wind serenade in C Minor, K. 388, created in 1782, for string quintet. He did this to combine it with the two quintets of 1787, K. 515 and K. 516, in order to offer a set of three for sale as a subscription, which he advertised in the *Wiener Zeitung* in April. Because of poor demand, Mozart extended the offer to January 1789.

When he was not teaching or composing, Mozart conducted a variety of performances, including a number for the Society of the Associated Gentlemen under the aegis of Baron van Swieten, who had remained in Vienna as a government official and continued to act as Mozart's appreciative and supportive patron. In February and March 1788, Mozart conducted C.P.E. Bach's "The Resurrection and Ascension of Jesus" at Count Johann Esterházy's residence and at the Burgtheater, with additional instrumentation, K. Anh. 109g (537d). He also played piano at a concert at the Venetian ambassador's residence in February and participated in a concert given by Mme. Duschek in April. And he provided additional orchestration with winds and conducted performances of Handel's *Acis and Galatea* (K. 566), *Messiah* (K. 572), *Alexander's Feast* (K. 591) and *Ode for St. Cecilia's Day*, (K. 592), all between 1788 and 1790.

During the winter and spring of 1788, he was also busy preparing the staging of *Don Giovanni* in Vienna. He was obliged to make changes because of the demands or perhaps the limitations of the members of the Viennese cast. The changes consisted of two new arias ("Dalla sue pace", K. 540a, and "In quali eccess ... Mi tradi", K 540c) and a new scene "Per queste due manine", K. 540b.

The emperor continued to follow the preparations, even while with his armies at the front, and was concerned that the music might prove too difficult. His fears, however, were unfounded. The opera opened in Vienna on May 7, 1788, and was a considerable success, pleasing both the public and the connoisseurs, such as Count Johann Carl von Zinzendorf. It was performed six times in May and eight more times during the balance of the year. However, despite his interest in the production, the emperor never attended a performance; he didn't return to the capital until December, and then in failing health from an exhausting and difficult campaign. It's quite likely however, that Mozart acquainted him with the work by singing and playing the score on the piano. He was paid 225 florins for the revisions to the opera.

Mozart composed other vocal music during 1788: the aria "Ah se in ciel, benigne stele" for Aloisia Lange, K. 538; "Ich möchte wohl der Kaiser sein", K. 539, a war song for bass Friedrich Baumann; an aria "Un bacio di mano", K. 541, for Francesco Albertarelli—the Don Giovanni of the Viennese production; for insertion into Pasquale Anfossi's opera *La gelosia fortunate*; another war song for children, "Dem hochen Kaiser-Worte treu (Lied beim Auszug in das Feld)", K.552; a *canzonetta* for three voices with brass accompaniment, K.549, and ten canons for four voices, K. 553 – K. 562. The canons included music based on common and coarse subjects, some in Viennese dialect, and others that were more exalted, such as K. 553, which was based on a Gregorian chant.

Despite this tremendous output, Mozart seemed unable to remain on a stable financial footing and in the middle of June 1788, less than six months after moving to a central location, he moved again to the suburb of Alsergrund to try to contain his expenses. He rationalized the move by convincing himself that more peaceful surroundings and a garden would allow him to compose more effectively; he could, after all, cheaply hire a carriage when he needed to go into town. Anxious about his economic problems, he approached a fellow Mason, businessman Michael Puchberg, for help. Between June 1788 and April 1791, Mozart wrote a series of nearly twenty letters to Puchberg, asking for loans. The first four were written in June and July 1788, requesting a loan of between 1,000 and 2,000 guldens, which would have allowed him to consolidate his finances and work more effectively, without the daily worry of meeting ongoing expenses. Puchberg instead advanced him a modest sum and Mozart continued his supplications for varying amounts to make ends meet.

Meanwhile, in his suburban home Mozart continued an outpouring of compositions. Over a period of six months, he produced his last three great symphonies, several chamber works, some vocal pieces and dances and arranged his fugue, originally for piano duet (K. 426 in C Minor), for strings with an added *adagio*, K.546. It is not known why Mozart composed the three symphonies. One of his letters suggests that he might have intended them for a series of concerts, but it has been also suggested by Küster that they might originally have been written for an ambitious publication plan by one of the companies to present works illustrating Mozart's mature musicianship together with other compositions, particularly of the chamber variety.

The chamber works of the period include another set of three piano trios: in E Major, K. 542, in C Major, K. 548, and in G Major, K. 564 (the last of these was composed in October). These piano trios share some characteristics with Mozart's symphonies; they contain *concertante* passages and provide all instruments with independent roles. Other compositions included a piano sonata in C Major, K. 545, a sonata for violin and piano in F Major, K. 547, and the magnificent string trio in E flat Major, K 563, for violin, viola and cello in six movements, which was completed in September. Mozart referred to it as a *divertimento* and could have composed it for Puchberg.

The symphonies (K. 543 in E flat Major, K. 550 in G Minor and K. 551 in C Major—"The Jupiter") represent the pinnacle of this genre in the eighteenth century. They contain a variety of musical ideas with various orchestral complements, tragic and dramatic tensions, as well as joyful and exalting moods. The *finale* of the last symphony provides a triumphant ending with unexcelled complexity of five themes, intertwined in a fugal counterpoint. There is little doubt that the symphonies were performed, but not until the following concert season (1788–1789) or possibly later. Mozart may have thought that the symphonies would draw the public to his concerts, after having a fill of his piano concertos. It appears however, that though more than a dozen advertisements for his works appeared in 1788, neither the concerts nor the publications significantly eased his financial woes.

In the last three months of the year, Mozart arranged and conducted Handel's *Acis and Galatea* for Baron van Swieten's group, as well as at his own benefit concert. Otherwise he composed only three sets of dances, perhaps in part because soon after the move to the suburbs, Wolfgang and Constanze's baby daughter died. This tragedy and the family's economic problems must have been a considerable burden. Yet, according to an actor from the Royal Copenhagen Theatre, who visited the Mozarts in their suburban home, their lives were filled with a quiet charm. The actor, as quoted by Gutman, wrote:

> This small man and great master improvised twice on a pianoforte with pedal and so wonderfully, that it staggered belief! He interwove the most difficult passages with the loveliest themes. His wife cut quills for the copyist, a pupil composed, and a little boy of four (Carl) walked about the garden singing recitatives. In short, everything surrounding this splendid man was musical.

Visitors often spoke thus of Mozart, in an almost religious manner. More than twenty performances of his operas were given during the year in Vienna and other cities. Also, more than a dozen advertisements of his music appeared during the year. They included music from *Don Giovanni*, recently composed arias and songs, dances, the piano concerto in G Major, K. 453, the duets for violin and viola, K. 423 and K. 424, the string trio, K. 563, three piano trios: K. 502, K. 542 and K. 548, and the clarinet trio, K.498, advertised both in Vienna and in Paris. In short, Mozart was a celebrity.

During the first three months of 1789, Mozart composed a piano sonata in B flat Major, K. 570, likely as teaching material, a set of six German dances, K. 571, and re-orchestrated Handel's *Messiah*, which he conducted at Count Johann Esterházy's. Though his financial difficulties likely continued, Mozart had not written to Puchberg for help since the previous July. Then an opportunity arose for Mozart to explore possible sources of earnings abroad. At the end of March, he wrote to a friend, Franz Hofdemel, and borrowed from him 100 gulden until his next salary installment, which was due later in April. In retrospect, the loan was probably intended to provide funds for an upcoming trip.

Prince Karl von Lichnowsky, a future patron of Beethoven, had undertaken to travel through Bohemia and visit Dresden and Leipzig en route to the Prussian capital in Berlin and the king's residence in Potsdam. Apparently he invited an eager Mozart to join him and presumably covered a lion's share of the expenses. After leaving Vienna on April 8th, they spent less than a day in Prague. There Mozart visited Franz Xaver Duschek whose wife, the singer Josepha, was in Dresden, and discussed the possibility of writing another opera for Prague with the new manager of the National Theatre, Dominico Guardasoni. Though Mozart wrote to his wife that Guardasoni "all but promised me 200 ducats for the opera and 50 ducats for travel expenses", there was in fact no firm offer.

The travellers proceeded to Dresden, arriving on the 12th and staying until the 18th. Mozart's presence in the city created both excitement and musical activity, and led to an impromptu concert at which a trio, either the string trio K. 563 or the piano trio K 542 was played, while Mme. Duschek sang arias from Mozart's operas. Though Mozart had to resume his travels with Prince Lichnowsky, he squeezed in a visit to the court of the Elector of Saxony, Frederick Augustus III. There, he played his latest piano concerto in D Major, K. 537, which had been composed a year earlier, and likely conducted one of his three new symphonies. The elector responded with a handsome gift of a snuffbox filled with 100 ducats. Mozart also attended an opera by Italian composer Dominico Cimarosa, gave a concert at the palace of the Russian ambassador and played the church organ. He was probably rewarded for his performances.

Lichnowsky and Mozart then travelled to Leipzig, where Mozart improvised on the organ at the Thomaskirche, which was used by Johann Sebastian Bach. It is said that Mozart seemed awestruck as he inspected an unfamiliar manuscript of a motet by Bach. After three days in Leipzig, the travellers moved on to Potsdam, arriving on April 25th.

Mozart's stay in Prussia lasted until May 28th, but the visit was interrupted by a return to Leipzig from the 8th to the 17th of May. Only one independent document of Mozart's dealings with the Prussian court exists. It is an entry dated April 26th, advising that the king directed Mozart to apply for an audience through official channels—that is, through the supervisor of concerts, cellist Jean-Pierre Duport. While waiting for an audience, Mozart wisely composed a set of keyboard variations on a minuet by Duport, entering it in his thematic catalogue as K. 573.

The rest of this story is based primarily on Mozart's letters to his wife. In them, he relates that he was given a gift of 100 friedrichs d'or (about 800 gulden) by the King of Prussia, and implies that he was commissioned to compose six string quartets for the king, who played the cello, as well as six easy piano sonatas for Princess Fredericke.

There are also stories that Mozart attended a performance of *Eintführung aus dem Serail* in Berlin, as well as a concert by his former pupil, Johann Nepomuk Hummel, and that he was received with unbounded enthusiasm. An early biography of Mozart by Georg Nikolaus von Nissen, Constanze's second husband, reports that the king offered Mozart an annual salary of 3,000 thalers, but Mozart did not accept, perhaps because he felt himself bound by his contract with the emperor in Vienna. The strained relationship between Vienna and Berlin may also have played a part. Constanze confirmed this account forty years later to the visiting Novellos, claiming that the king himself had told her about the offer.

Despite these accounts, there are difficulties in determining what actually took place during the trip, or their significance, for there is a gap in the surviving letters that Mozart wrote to his wife. Four were written between April 8th and 16th. These were followed by an interval of a month before another four letters, written between May 16th and 31st, have been preserved. According to Mozart, his letters and those his wife wrote to him during the period were lost, but there is speculation that he may have had a romantic liaison with Mme. Duschek. His repeated assurances of his love and devotion in his correspondence with his wife suggest that she was concerned about his actions.

There seems to have been little reason for his second trip to Leipzig, which Mozart blamed on Prince Lichnowsky, who purportedly urged him to go back and give a concert. He relates that he gave a concert that was successful musically and included Mme Duschek, but was poorly attended and did not bring any significant earnings. Solomon expresses doubts that Mozart was ever received by the king, and wonders whether he might have borrowed money, perhaps from Lichnowsky, to be able to show something as the result of his trip. There have been suggestions that Mozart went on the trip because he needed to get away from Vienna, but most biographers accept the events as related in his letters.

Mozart returned to Vienna on June 4th, after brief stops in Dresden and Prague. He wrote to Constanze, asking her to meet him with friends and his son Carl at the city gates. His letters again tell her how he missed her, and express his love and anticipation of their reunion.

Soon after his return, Mozart began the works for the Prussian court. He finished the first string quartet for the king, in D Major, K. 575, in June, and a piano sonata in the same key, K. 576, for the princess in July. The quartet contains a considerable contribution by the cello, the king's chosen instrument. However, the piano sonata is anything but easy, with challenging contrapuntal passages. Mozart may have begun the next string quartet, but didn't complete it until the following May.

The interruption was likely due to his deteriorating financial situation, exacerbated by a serious threat to Constanze's health. In July 1789, Constanze was five months into her fifth pregnancy. She had developed an ulcer on her ankle, which refused to heal and became infected; the attending physicians were concerned that the underlying bone might be affected, a potentially dangerous situation.

Extensive ulcerations in the ankle region are a common complication of damage to the veins of the legs. This damage may result from complications related to pregnancies and childbirth. The ulcers are often large and difficult to heal; in fact, they may remain unhealed for years. Until recently, prolonged bed rest was the only effective treatment available. Only late in the twentieth century did special pressure dressings lead to a thera-peutic breakthrough.

In July, as Mozart's medical expenses mounted, his letters asking Puchberg for help resumed and soon grew desperate. Puchberg kept sending Mozart funds, which over three years amounted to nearly 1,500 gulden. He did not ask for repayment when Mozart died and it's possible that Mozart had repaid at least some of the monies. Despite lack of a definitive treat-ment, Constanze's condition slowly improved, probably thanks to simple bed rest. In August, she was able to take the baths in nearby Baden. Mozart wrote to her from Vienna and visited her in Baden; seeing her on the mend so improved his spirits that he was able to work again.

A focus of Mozart's activities that summer was the revival of his opera *Le Nozze di Figaro*, in Vienna. It was first staged on August 29th at the Burgtheater, a performance that the recovering Constanze was able to attend, and then performed ten more times during the remainder of the year. To accommodate the new singers, Mozart composed two replacement arias "Al desio, di chi T'adora", K. 577, and "Un moto di gioia", K. 579, and made other minor adjustments. During this period and later in the year, he also composed three individual soprano arias. These included "Alma grande e nobil core", K. 578, for his new Susanna, Adriana Ferrarese del Bene—an insertion to an opera by Domenico Cimarosa; two arias for insertion into Martin y Sorer's opera *Il barbiere di buon cuore*, "Chi sà qual sia", K. 582, and "Vado, ma dove?", K. 583, and in December, an aria "Rivolgete a lui lo sguardo" for his own next opera *Cosi fan tutte*, K. 584, which was later replaced.

Near the end of September, Mozart completed one of his most sublime compositions, the quintet for clarinet and string quartet in A Major, K. 581, for his friend and fellow Mason Anton Stadler, a superb virtuoso of that instrument. Stadler had an extension added to his instrument that extended the lower register and Mozart composed the quintet, as well as the clarinet concerto in 1791, for Stadler's instrument. In this work the part of the clarinet is balanced more evenly with the strings than in other chamber works that Mozart composed for wind instruments and strings. As pointed out by Küster, in the first movement the clarinet initially has a background role before coming to the fore. This balance seems to be comparable to that of the keyboard and of the string trio in Mozart's piano quartets of 1785 and 1786. Though written in the bright key of A Major, the quintet contains modulations to the darker minor modes and is full of melodies that tug at the heart strings.

As expressed by Robbins Landon, "The music smiles through the tears. It displays all the composer's love for and understanding of the clarinet …".

The prominent passages played by the strings alone give the clarinetist a respite of several measures in the first movement allegretto. After an intense and lyrical *larghetto*, in the *menuetto*, the clarinet is silent for seven measures during the minuet proper. Mozart includes two separate trios in this movement. The first of thirty-nine measures is for strings alone, and is repeated, giving the clarinet a longer respite. In the last movement, *allegretto con variazioni,* the clarinet blends almost imperceptibly with the strings in the theme and in the third variation before the final variation that consists of three parts. The first part contains a series of broken chord semiquavers played by the clarinet and is followed by a tremendously lyrical, almost painful, *adagio.* A brisk *allegro*, which quotes the opening theme, brings the work to a bright conclusion.

Stadler performed it during the Christmas concert of the Society of Viennese Musicians on December 22nd. Mozart had a high regard for Stadler's virtuosity and was on very friendly terms with him. However Stadler, who had a large family that he had difficulty supporting, took advantage of Mozart's friendship and generosity, swindled him and failed to repay a sizeable loan, which the composer could ill afford to lose.

In December, Mozart composed three sets of dances (minuets K. 585, German dances, K. 586, and a contredanse, K. 587). He was also already working on his opera *Cosi fan tutte,* and likely had been since October or even earlier in the year, as suggested by an analysis of the manuscript by Alan Tyson, co-editor of *Mozart's Thematic Catalogue: A*

Facsimile. The origins of this commission are a mystery. The work was first offered to Antonio Salieri, who abandoned it and the librettist da Ponte then turned to his favorite—Mozart. The opera was to be given early in 1790 and Mozart and da Ponte worked rapidly because of the shortage of time. Mozart wrote to Puchberg asking for a sizeable loan, based on the fee of 200 ducats that he expected for the opera and invited him to a rehearsal, probably to demonstrate that he was engaged in work that would bring a sizeable payment.

Though Mozart's works for publication were advertised several times during the year and his operas were performed nearly forty times in Vienna and other cities, these did not help his economic situation. His financial struggles may well have contributed to the strains in Mozart's marriage. There was clearly some mutual jealousy; Constanze was probably suspicious about her husband's activities during the trip to the Prussian court, and in his correspondence Mozart had lectured Constanze on her loose behaviour during her trip to Baden. He believed she had encouraged an officer whom she met there, though she was well advanced in her pregnancy. In November, Constanze gave birth to a daughter, who died shortly after birth.

The composition of *Cosi fan tutte* must have been approaching completion early in January, for the first orchestral rehearsal was held on the 21st with Haydn and Puchberg in attendance. The plot has two army officers testing the fidelity of their fiancées, who are sisters. The subject is derived from antiquity, but in writing the libretto, da Ponte used more recent sources, particularly *Orlando furioso* by Ludovico Ariosto. The officers, who believe the faithfulness of their beloveds, are lured to bet with a wise "philosopher", Alfonso. With the help of the sisters' maid Despina, Alfonso stages an apparent departure of the men to war. Military music was topical in Vienna at the time, because of the ongoing war with Turkey. At Alfonso's order, the officers, disguised as travelling Albanians, return and woo their fiancées, switching their partners. The ladies eventually give way, thus proving Alfonso right and the officers lose the bet. The women, their fickleness exposed when their fiancées unmask, are indignant and contrite, but the events are mutually forgiven and love appears to be restored. The opera ends with the six characters praising the man who is guided by reason and who will accept good and ill fortune alike, with philosophic calm.

Overall, the message of the opera is consistent with the ideas of the Enlightenment. Mozart, however, adds a disquieting twist by leaving the audience uncertain as to whether the feelings the lovers had for one another have been restored.

The opera opened on January 26th and was successful, certainly musically. However, after five performances the emperor, Mozart's supporter, died on February 20th and the performances were suspended. Four more performances were given after the period of mourning ended later in the year.

Various aspects of the plot raised controversies, which have been debated ever since. These questions included how the women could not have recognized their disguised fiancées, a criticism similar to that of the walking and talking statue of the Commendatore in *Don Giovanni*. The demeaning of women raised concerns and apologetic statements were made before some performances. However, men's unfaithfulness is mentioned in the opera as well. The authors' message appears to be the reality of human frailties and the need to understand and accept it.

In creating the opera, Mozart could have been affected by his own experiences with Constanze's jealousy and his recurring concerns about her flirtatious nature. This was not something new; playing a game during their courtship, she had allowed her calves to be measured by another man. That event recalled a similar situation involving Mozart during one of his Italian trips, though according to his correspondence, he had apparently resisted successfully. Whether the opera related to Mozart's marital life at the time is uncertain. Decades later, Constanze told the visiting Novellos that she did not care for the plot, but that that the music carried the work.

Emperor Joseph's death unsettled the Viennese court and altered Mozart's position. Mozart's supporter, Baron van Swieten, apparently did not enjoy the favour of the new emperor, Leopold II, nor did Salieri, who was later replaced as the court's Kappelmeister. Mozart petitioned to be given the post of second Kappelmeister, but was confirmed in his original position. His relationship with the new emperor was remote and perhaps as a result, Mozart was not very active musically during the initial months following Emperor Joseph's death. On April 9th, he participated in a concert at Count Hadik's during which his string trio, K. 563, and the clarinet quintet were played. His operas *Figaro* and *Cosi* were again performed at the Burgtheater from May until October, and Mozart conducted at least one of the performances. In May, he completed the second Prussian string quartet in B flat Major, K. 589, and in June the third of the set in F Major, K. 590. In July, he reworked Handel's *Ode to St. Cecilia's Day* and *Alexander's Feast* for Baron van Swieten, and in August composed the duet "Nun, liebes Wiebchen", K. 625, for Schikaneder's play, *Der Stein der Weisen*, ("The Philosopher's Stone").

He also took on more pupils, but his economic problems continued, as evidenced by ten letters to Puchberg written between December 29, 1789 and August 5, 1790. And once again the medical expenses mounted, as doctors prescribed another set of cures in Baden for Constanze near the end of May.

Musical activities resumed at the court in Vienna in September, with various royal visitors arriving for weddings in the emperor's family. Plans for upcoming coronations were also being formulated, but Mozart was not invited to participate. Desperate to show his abilities to the new emperor, as well as to boost his earnings, he suddenly decided to travel to the coronation in Frankfurt on his own and give concerts there and in other cities. He pawned the family silver to cover the expenses, bought a comfortable carriage, and on September 24th set out with his brother-in-law, the violinist Hofer, for Frankfurt.

Arriving on the 28th, he remained there until October 16th, during which time he wrote several letters to his wife. In them, he discussed his financial affairs and gave accounts of his activities, which included attending various performances and meeting with a banker. With the help of Constanze, who was recovering well, a loan of 1,000 gulden at the rate of five per cent was arranged with Heinrich Lackenbacher to help Mozart consolidate his finances and allow him to work with peace of mind. During his absence, Constanze moved with six-year-old Carl to a cheaper apartment.

Despite his considerable efforts, Mozart did not take part in any of the activities associated with the emperor's coronation, which took place on October 9th. Instead, he arranged his own concert six days later, which included one of his symphonies and a personal performance of his piano concertos K. 459 and K. 537. Though musically successful, the concert was a financial failure. The appreciative audience was small, largely because of other events going on simultaneously. The day after his concert, Mozart travelled to Mainz, where he performed at the Court of the Archbishop on October 20th. He left the next day for Mannheim to attend the first German performance of *Figaro*; after two days he continued on through Augsburg to Munich. There he renewed his acquaintance with the Cannabichs, Ramm and others who had played prominent roles during his trip thirteen years earlier.

The Elector Karl Theodore, for whom he had composed *Idomeneo* a decade before, summoned him to perform in early November in front of guests, including the king and queen of Naples, who were returning from the coronation. Mozart likely obtained a handsome fee for this performance before setting out at last for Vienna, arriving on November 10th.

Proceeding for the first time to his new residence, he found that his wife had done well. The apartment was comfortable and well decorated with a large study, a billiard room, a sitting room and a large living room. Moreover, the courtyard had room to store Mozart's carriage. After a long journey that had yielded at best mediocre financial reward, and during which he composed only one work, an *adagio* and *allegro* for a mechanical organ, K. 594, he must have found the surroundings comforting.

There were some positive omens during the last few weeks of 1790. The first was a letter from an impresario in England, inviting him to come in December to compose two operas over six months for a fee equivalent to 2,400 guldens. In addition, Mozart could earn fees from giving concerts. Soon another English concert manager, Johann Peter Salomon, arrived in Vienna to invite Haydn and Mozart to come and produce music for generous fees. Haydn accepted and went to London, where he was very successful. Mozart opted to remain in Vienna; it seems Constanze could not accompany him without concerns for her health and he seems to have been reluctant to leave her again. However, Salomon made it clear that the generous offer would be available to him at a later date.

In December, Mozart composed the string quintet in D Major, K. 593, likely on a commission from John Tost, a former member of Haydn's orchestra who had come into money through marriage. A much brighter composition than his quintets of 1787, the new quintet was close in style to the music of Haydn, a tribute to his esteemed friend. However, as was typical, Mozart put his own stamp on the work. Uniquely he used a *larghetto–allegro–larghetto–allegro* pattern in the first movement and ended the work with an inspiring contrapuntal *finale*. Along with his earlier quintets, this work was played in Mozart's apartment in December, with Haydn alternating the first and second viola parts with him.

Clearly concerned about Haydn's ability to get along abroad, Mozart spent a good deal of time with him prior to his departure on December 15th. "Papa!" he said, for that is how he referred to his old friend, "you have no education for the great world, and you speak too few languages."

During their farewell dinner, tears came to Mozart's eyes. "We are probably saying our last adieu in this life," he said. And indeed they would not see one another again, for Mozart died a year later. It apparently did not occur to either of them that the older man would outlive his younger friend.

Chapter 8

A Brief Renewal and Unexpected Tragedy

Mozart's compositional output, which had slowed uncharacteristically in 1790, rebounded strongly in the New Year. In the first half of January, he composed three songs for children commissioned by the bookseller Ignaz Alberti: "Komm, lieber Mai" ("Come, glad month of May"), K. 596, "Erwacht zum neuen Leben" ("Awake to new life"), K. 597, and "Wir Kinder, wir schmecken der Freuden recht viel" ("We children, taste many joys"), K. 598. The texts of the songs, all in major keys, and the music were joyful and dealt with spring. Metaphorically, this new beginning went hand-in-hand with Mozart's renewed flurry of activities. Prior to composing the songs, he had entered a new piano concerto, no. 27 in B flat Major, K. 595, in his catalogue. Though he had sketched the outline of the work a couple of years earlier, he now completed it, using the thematic material of the first of the three songs in the last movement *rondo*. Gutman wrote that though the concerto speaks in simpler musical language than previous concertos, its high sensibility and beauty, as well as elements of the monumental, make it characteristic of Mozart's other works of the period. He probably played the new concerto at the public benefit concert for clarinetist Joseph Bäer on March 4th.

By March 6th, Mozart had fulfilled his duties as a court composer, producing a total of twelve minuets, fourteen German dances, and nine contredances, K. 599 – K. 607 and K. 611, in various sets. The orchestral complements varied. Some included hurdy-gurdy or sleighbells (K. 605), but all were of high quality and made Mozart the most famous composer of ballroom music at the time. By March, Artaria had advertised several of these compositions in the *Wiener Zeitung.*

Most of these compositions were for the balls at the Redout-ensaal. Dancing had gained great popularity in Vienna during the 1780s. The balls at the Redoutensaal represented the culmination of the year's dance activities. They were held during Carnival season and, as a result of the liberal reforms of Emperor Joseph II, were attended by all ranks of society. The mixing of classes was facilitated by the use of masks, which concealed an individual's identity. Mozart himself was very fond of dancing and the Mozarts and their friends attended many balls during their years in Vienna.

Mozart then turned to composing in other genres. A fantasia in F Minor for mechanical organ, K. 608, entered his catalogue in March and was followed in May by an *andante* in F Major, K. 616, for the same instrument. Mozart composed several works in April: the aria "Per questa bella mano", K. 612, for the bass singer Franz Gerl, who was to sing the role of Sarastro in "The Magic Flute", with a solo part for the principal double bassist Friedrich Pichelberger (both were members of Emanuel Schikaneder's troupe then in residence at the Theater auf der Wieden, in a Viennese suburb), and a string quintet in E flat Major, K. 614, a companion to his D Major quintet, K. 593, composed in late 1790. Like its predecessor, K. 614 was created in the style of Joseph Haydn and is thought to have been a part of the commission for Johann Tost.

Mozart also composed a vocal quartet "Viviamo Felice", K. 615, for insertion into the opera *Le gelosie villane* by Italian conductor and composer Guiseppe Sarti, which unfortunately has been lost. On May 23rd, an *adagio* and *rondo* for glass armonica with flute, oboe, viola and cello, K. 617, was completed for Marianne Kirchgässner, a blind virtuoso on this remarkable and briefly fashionable instrument. (An *adagio* in C Major, K. 356/617b, for the same instrument was also composed in 1791.)

THE GLASS ARMONICA

THIS INSTRUMENT, which is remarkable both in its invention and its sound, had its beginnings with an Irishman, Richard Pockridge, who performed on what he called an "angelic organ"—a set of tuned wine glasses filled with water. After perfecting a repertoire that included Handel's Water Music, he took his talents on tour. Though Pockridge, and his instrument, perished in a fire in 1759, prior to his death his music inspired others, including Edmund Delaval. A member of the Royal Society in London, Delaval created his own "angelic organ" and played it for friends and colleagues. Among them was *Benjamin Franklin*, the prodigious American inventor, who was living in London in 1761, working as a lobbyist for the Pennsylvania colonial legislature.

Inspired, Franklin—who was passionate about music—determined to create his own instrument and in the process improve on the original. In his 1991 biography, Benjamin Franklin, Carl Van Doren quoted the inventor thusly: "Being charmed by the sweetness of its tones and the music he produced from it, I wished only to see the glasses disposed in a more convenient form ..."

Franklin asked a glassmaker to create thirty-seven half-spheres made of glass, diminishing in size and thickness so as to nest inside one another horizontally. Linked with an iron rod, the spheres were held in place with cork, and the instrument was powered by a foot treadle, which turned a wheel and the rod itself. With the glass spheres spinning, Franklin moistened his fingers and, holding them to the rims of the colour coded spheres, produced sounds that were just short of heavenly.

Franklin quickly mastered the instrument, which he called his "glass armonica" and in 1761 began taking it to dinner parties. It was an almost instant hit. Thousands were soon being produced and sold and the armonica became a fashionable topic of conversation. Even Marie-Antoinette studied and played the instrument.

Mozart first heard it in 1773, on tour in Vienna with his father, but though more than 300 pieces were written for the instrument between 1765 and 1820, Mozart's two pieces for the armonica were not composed until 1791, the year he died. Both were written for virtuoso Marianne Kirchgessner, who toured Europe with the instrument. The majority of players were women, but composers were overwhelmingly male, including Beethoven, Richard Strauss and Camille Saint-Saëns.

Ben Franklin played until he died in 1790 and said his "beloved Armonica" gave him more pleasure than anything else. The instrument's popularity died as quickly as it was born, but today has again found a following among musicians interested in period instruments.

A Glass Armonica

Joshua Stanton, 2005

In April 1791, Mozart submitted a petition for an unpaid position at St. Stephen's Cathedral as assistant to the aging Kappelmeister Hoffmann, with the understanding that he would take over from him after he died. This was granted in May. Early in June, Constanze who was eight months pregnant, went to Baden with six-year-old Carl. Mozart sent his student Franz Xaver Süssmayr to assist his wife; he also visited her several times and they corresponded frequently. During one of his visits in June, Mozart composed the eerily beautiful and celebrated motet "Ave, verum corpus", K. 618, for choir, strings and organ. The composition was probably for the local church musician Anton Stoll, for performance on Corpus Christi. In mid-July, Mozart composed a cantata, "Die ihr des unermesslichen Weltalls Schöpfer ehrt", K. 619, for tenor and keyboard, which had been commissioned by a fellow Mason. Then he brought Constanze back to Vienna, where on July 26th she gave birth to their sixth child, a son, Franz Xaver Wolfgang.

Mozart, meanwhile, was hard at work on three major compositions. In the spring, he'd begun composing a new opera, *Die Zauberflöte* ("The Magic Flute") with Emanuel Schikaneder, a fellow Freemason, actor, playwright and impresario, writing the text. Mozart had met him in 1780 when Schikaneder was in Salzburg with a travelling troupe. Schikaneder had leased the Theater auf der Wieden in a Viennese suburb and, catering to the wider public, put on a variety of concerts and performances in German. He built an elaborate stage set, complete with machinery for spectacular effects, and provided lighting along a road from the city, so that his patrons, including members of the court and nobility, could safely attend his performances.

During the summer of 1791, Mozart obtained two other commissions for major works: an *opera seria, La clemeza di Tito,* for the coronation of the new emperor in Prague in September, and a requiem for Count Franz von Walsegg-Stuppach, to commemorate the death of his young wife in February. The count had the quaint habit of commissioning works and passing them off as his own compositions played by his resident musicians.

Mozart must have felt at home working with Schikaneder and his group, for the troupe included Constanze's sister Josepha as the main soprano, and two male singers—tenor Benedikt Schak and bass Franz Gerl —who, according to Constanze, became Mozart's close friends. Mozart had previously composed piano variations in F Major, K. 613, on a theme by one of them in a play *Der dumme Gärtner* ("The Stupid Gardner"), provided the orchestration for the duet, K. 625, for Schikaneder's singspiel, *Der Stein der Weisen* ("The Philosopher's Stone") and an aria for Gerl, K. 612.

 Die Zauberflöte was a German play with spoken dialogue and musical numbers, corresponding to a singspiel, though Mozart referred to it as a grand opera, likely because of its stylistic diversity. The libretto had elements from several sources. The plot begins as Prince Tamino is given a "magic flute" and undertakes to rescue the Queen of the Night's daughter Pamina from the evil sorcerer Sarastro. He is accompanied by the comic birdman Papageno (played by Schikaneder). In the second act, the story switches to elements of the initiation rites of ancient Egypt. The evil Sarastro becomes a just and wise man and the Queen of the Night a wicked sorceress. The sources for the libretto included a story, "Lulu oder die Zauberflüte", by Jacub August Liebeskind, and the opera *Oberon* by Czech composer Paul Wranizky, which had been performed by Schikaneder's company. There were also elements of music from Mozart's previous works, particularly *Thamos, König in Ägypten*, K. 345, which was based on a play by Mason Franz Gebler, begun in 1773 in Vienna and later revised in Salzburg. The play in turn, was derived from a French novel, *Sethos*, by Abbé Jean Terrasson, written in 1731 and dealing with Egyptian initiation rites and other experiences of a young prince who assumes the throne from his benevolent father.

The rescue of Pamina harkens back to the *Eintführung's* rescue of Konstanze, reflecting the ideas of Enlightment and equality of women, though here Mozart departed from Masonic custom—the Masons did not allow women in their order. The benevolence of Sarastro follows a similar act of forgiveness of the Sultan Soliman in the unfinished opera fragment *Zaide,* K. 344, composed in Salzburg in 1779-1780, of Selim Pasha in the *Eintführung* and of Idomeneo. The Egyptian initiation rites were a thin disguise for Masonic rituals. The music and the play contain Masonic elements of multiple threes: three boys, three ladies of the queen, three chords that open the overture and sound at the end of the march of the priests, and three flats in the key of E flat. The music is a rich mixture of bright numbers for Papageno, bravura arias of the Queen of the Night, a Handelian duet, and hymn-like sections reminiscent of Bach and of Mozart's own Masonic music.

By mid-July, the score of "The Magic Flute" was nearing completion. Approached with commissions for the requiem and for *La Clemenza di Tito*, Mozart accepted. There was an advance fee for the requiem, which Mozart needed, and he undoubtedly felt that an opera for the coronation in Prague might put him in a good light with the new emperor, who had shown little interest in him. The opera was most urgent; Mozart had only six weeks to compose it. The work had initially been offered to Salieri, who declined, and the Bohemian impresario Guardasoni then turned to Mozart. The libretto was derived from work by eighteenth-century Italian poet and librettist Pietro Metastasio and originally performed with music in 1734. However, it had not been performed since 1774 and needed updating. With Lorenzo da Ponte gone to London, the Dresden poet Caterino Mazolà was summoned to undertake the task.

The story glorifies the splendid, benevolent ruler Titus, in whom the audiences of the eighteenth-century Austria would see their respective rulers. In 1791, the new Emperor Leopold, with his record of benevolent rule in Florence, embodied Titus. It was in many ways an apt comparison, for Leopold was a follower of Enlightment tenets and his reign had several parallels with that of Titus. Mazolà streamlined and updated the libretto, emphasizing the three main characters and clearly outlining the disasters that Titus had to overcome. Having survived these trials, Titus then reigned with benevolence.

Faced with very tight deadlines, Mozart worked feverishly, aided by his student Süssmayer. On August 25th, he left for Prague with his wife and Süssmayer, working in the coach as he travelled. Needless to say, the opera was composed in a hurry. While the result might have been different had time allowed Mozart to rely less on his student for recitatives and to put more effort into the music, the work nevertheless contains Mozartean beauty and character. These are exemplified by the arias with obbligato for clarinet and basset horn, which were played by Stadler. And during the coronation ceremonies, Salieri conducted several masses and other works composed by Mozart.

On the second of September, Mozart conducted a performance of *Don Giovanni*, which had likely been requested by the court, and on the sixth, the première of *La Clemenza* was given. The audience for the initial performance consisted mainly of court members and guests and it was obvious that the royal family was not impressed. By comparison, the last performance, held on September 30th and attended by the people of Prague, was much appreciated. Alas, Mozart was not there to witness the accolades; he had left about mid-month for Vienna, where a busy schedule awaited.

His most immediate task was to compose the remaining parts of "The Magic Flute": the march of the priests and the overture. This done, Mozart conducted the première on September 30th. The opera at once became a resounding success with both connoisseurs and commoners. It was performed two dozen times over the next five weeks and became a favourite throughout Germany and well beyond for years to come. Mozart attended the performances and related the reception to Constanze in his letters to her in Baden, where she had resumed her bath cures. He took his son, his mother-in-law and Salieri and his mistress to the performances and was pleased with Salieri's enthusiastic praise.

While revelling in the success of "The Magic Flute", Mozart turned to other compositions, including the requiem and a clarinet concerto for Stadler's basset clarinet. Using a fragment of the first movement of a concerto for basset horn that he'd sketched a couple of years earlier, he modified it for the basset clarinet, adding a slow movement in 3/4 time and an exuberant *rondo*. Küster points to modulation of minor keys in the opening movements of the concerto, similar to those of the clarinet quintet, which were both written for Stadler's special instrument. The modulation darkens the mood, greatly enhancing the beauty of the music. Mozart's musical genius shines in this magnificent work.

Mozart's letters to his wife during early October exude his vigour and zest for life. He has a good appetite, plays billiards and works

The playbill
for the first
performances
of "The Magic
Flute", Mozart's
last and peren-
nially popular
opera.

hard. He is also concerned with the quality of education that his son Carl is receiving at the boarding school and considers a change. The major portion of his time was now spent working furiously on the requiem. In one letter to Constanze, he mentions that he began writing one morning and did not stop until 1:30 A.M.

By the time he left to bring his wife home in mid-October, he had composed the *Kyrie*, and begun the *Introit* and possibly additional movements. According to Constanze, she took him for a carriage ride in the parkland of Prater on October 21ˢᵗ or 22ⁿᵈ. During the outing, Mozart told her that he believed he was writing the requiem for himself and that he was going to die soon. Alarmed, Constanze called a doctor and took the score from Wolfgang, convinced it was depressing him.

This account is at variance with Mozart's otherwise good humour at the time. He composed a Masonic cantata "Laut verkündeunsere Freude", K. 623, for performance at the lodge, Zur neugekrönte Hoffnung, for two tenors, bass and orchestra, which he conducted on November 18ᵗʰ. This composition, dated November 15ᵗʰ, was the last Mozart entered in his thematic catalogue.

His mood buoyed by the success of the cantanta, he returned to work on the requiem, which Constanze had given back to him. He completed the *Introit* and in draft score *Kyrie*, sequence:"Dies irae", Tuba mirum", "Rex tremendae", "Recordare", "Confutatis", and eight bars of "Lacrimosa", as well as the *Offertory*: "Domine Jesu" and "Hostias", which needed to be fully orchestrated. Even the partial score of the requiem in Mozart's hand amounts to ninety-nine sheets, an amazing feat in slightly more than a month.

In the middle of November, Prince Lichnowsky, Mozart's fellow Mason and companion during his 1789 trip to Germany, sued Mozart for a sizeable debt, probably related to the expenses of their trip. The provincial tribunal issued a writ against Mozart, which was probably never executed. The prince's action might have been prompted by the appearance of Mozart's improving finances. There were fees from the operas, new commissions and offers of support from patrons abroad, as well as proceeds from publications. Artaria and other publishers were advertising music from "The

Magic Flute" and other works in the *Wiener Zeitung* in November.

Two days after conducting the Masonic cantata, Mozart fell ill and took to his bed. Though his wife, sister-in-law Sophie and several pupils tended to his needs, his joints were soon swollen and painful and he was apparently aware that he was going to die. He was bitterly disappointed at leaving his family in financial difficulties, particularly since his circumstances were finally improving as his fame grew, and opportunities beckoned. Mozart's health and this final illness are studied in greater detail in Part II.

He was unable to continue to compose, though in addition to the requiem, he had other works in progress. These included a concerto for horn for his friend Leutgeb in D Major, K. 412 + 514. He had finished only the first movement; Süssmayer completed the second the following year, using Mozart's sketches. According to a list that Constanze later prepared, there were nearly 100 fragments that Mozart left unfinished. Though some would undoubtedly have been abandoned, others would have been used in further work had Mozart survived his illness.

Alan Tyson, co-editor of Mozart's thematic catalogue, considers that among his works in progress in the latter part of 1791, the composer was working on a violin sonata, a string trio, a string quintet and another mass; all this demonstrates the continued vitality of his muse. Whether he discussed the completion of the requiem with Süssmayer is uncertain. Despite, or possibly because of the efforts of his physician, he succumbed in the early hours of December 5th, 1791. His wife was distraught and inconsolable. Wanting to contract his illness and die, she threw herself on Mozart's body, as he lay in his bed. She was led away with her son to the home of friends.

Mourners paid their respects. Shikaneder did what he could to assist the devastated family and Mozart's longtime friend and supporter Baron van Swieten came to help with the arrangements for a third-class funeral, the most common type at the time. The baron did this despite the fact that on the same day he had received notice that he had been dismissed from his position as the president of the Court Commission for Education. He may also have helped Constanze in other ways, as she set out about providing for the bereft family.

On December 6th, after receiving the final blessing at the

Cathedral of St. Stephen, the funeral procession proceeded to the city gates. From there the coffin was taken in a carriage to the Cemetery of St. Marx in the Viennese suburb and buried in a normal single grave. The burial may have taken place on the 7th; regulations at the time called for a period of forty-eight hours after death before burial. Also, an account of rain and snow on the day of the burial fits the record of the weather on the 7th. December 6th had been a mild, calm day. The day after Mozart died, the *Wiener Zeitung* referred to his death as an "irreplaceable loss" and on the 13th, a service at St. Michael's was held during which the completed parts of the requiem were performed.

Common graves were unmarked at the time and that was the case with that of Mozart's. Because of a shortage of space, graves were cleared after about seven years and reused. Though Constanze wrote in Mozart's album "… we were united by the tenderest of bonds never to be severed here below! Oh! Soon may I join you forever," she did not visit the cemetery until about seventeen years after her husband's death. In a letter written less than a year before she died in 1842, she said that she did not follow the procession to the cemetery because of her pain, illness and the hard winter. By the time she did visit, she was told that the place was unknown. The lack of a special burial and a proper memorial might be ascribed to the reality that Mozart was not a favourite of his rival musicians at the imperial court, nor of Emperor Leopold II and his empress, and there was not enough will among his admirers to mount a necessary effort at the time. This indifference was pointed out within a few years after his death and it is said that Joseph Haydn complained bitterly about it.

Attempts to locate Mozart's final resting place took place more than fifty years after his death. According to Anton Neumayr, an 1845 account in *Kleine Wiener Memoires,* by a Franz Gräffer, stated that the gravedigger at St. Marx knew exactly where Mozart was buried, and that an elderly widow of a musician came every year to pray at the grave. She was the widow of Johan Georg Albrechtsberger, a composer and friend of Mozart. He died in 1809, but previously had been given Mozart's position as assistant at St. Stephen's Cathedral and eventually became its Kappelmeister, a position that Mozart hoped to obtain before he died. The veracity of that information was apparently confirmed by Karl Hirsch, Alberchtsberger's grandson, who accompanied his grandmother on the visits to the cemetery where they prayed at the sites of the burial of the two composers. Karl continued to visit the cemetery and knew the location of Mozart's burial. Hermine Cloeter, as quoted by Neumayr, reports that a common tailor planted a willow tree to mark the site and subsequently, in 1859, Viennese authorities erected a monument sculpted by Hans Gasser, on the site after an investigation in 1841. This monument was transferred to Vienna's main municipal cemetery on the occasion of the 100th anniversary of Mozart's death in 1891. The site might have been lost for good then but for a cemetery caretaker, Alexander Kugler, who put together a "monument" made of parts of various memorials, including an angel and a broken column, in the area where the composer was buried. That memorial survived World War II and a photo appears in Neumayr's *Music and Medicine.*

Whether or not the account by Neumayr is true is uncertain. Today a monument (shown above), designed by sculptor Florian Josephu-Drouot in 1950 and featuring a broken column and an angel with a sad face, marks at least an approximate location where the remains of one of the greatest geniuses of mankind were buried.

In another twist, a skull claimed to be Mozart's surfaced during the nineteenth century and has been kept at the Mozarteum in Salzburg since the early twentieth century. In the autumn of 2004, excavations of the Mozart-Nissen gravesite in Salzburg were carried out to obtain DNA samples of the members of Mozart's family (father, grandmother and niece) and possibly Mozart's sister, who was buried elsewhere. If these should be found to have a common DNA, then the comparison could be done with the DNA of the skull to determine whether or not it is genuine. Various previous examinations leave considerable doubt that it is Mozart's.

After Mozart died, Constanze worked hard to provide for herself and her two sons. In time, she met a Danish diplomat, Georg Nissen, who marriedher in 1809 and took on the role of caring husband and father.

Mozart's two sons, Franz, left, and Carl, both died childless, thus ending Mozart's direct geneological line. The extended family, descended from his uncle, Josef Ignaz, continued into the twentieth century. The last member of the line apparently died in Augsburg in 1965.

IMAGNO / Austrian Archives

After he retired from the diplomatic service, he worked on Mozart's biography. In 1820, they settled in Salzburg, where Nannerl also lived.

The relationship between Mozart's sister and his widow has aroused considerable debate, fuelled in part by a letter sent by Nannerl to assist with a biography of her brother. It contained a passage that may not have been written by her, which implied that Constanze was not a suitable wife for Wolfgang. However, it is likely the relationship, while not close, was reasonably cordial. Mozart's younger son, Franz Xaver Wolfgang, was very attentive to his aunt whenever he visited Salzburg, according to the Novellos, who met him when they visited the city shortly before Nannerl died in 1829. The Novellos also reported at least one visit by Constanze to her sister-in-law. In her will, Nannerl left many of her father's letters to Constanze, and Nannerl's son, Leopold, who inherited from his mother some family items, was instructed by her that the items should pass to her brother's sons after Leopold's death. Young Leopold, however, handed the items to Wolfgang's sons soon after the death of his mother.

Constanze's sisters, Aloisia, with whom Mozart fell in love during his trip to Paris, and Sophie, who tended to his needs during his final illness, joined her in Salzburg. All three sisters died there between 1839 and 1846. Mozart's father's grave in St. Sebastian's churchyard was opened to add several others, including Genoveva Weber, Constanze's aunt and mother of the composer Carl Maria von Weber, Nannerl's daughter Jeannette, and Constanze and her second husband Nissen. Aloisia and Sophie were also buried in St. Sebastian's cemetery. Nannerl, who had originally planned to be buried next to her father, changed her mind shortly after Constanze's husband was buried nearby. A codicil to her will stipulated that she be buried in St. Peter's churchyard.

After giving up music, Mozart's elder son Carl became an official at the court in Milan and died there in 1858. His brother Franz became a musician and composer and spent many years in Lemberg before returning to Vienna. The Novellos, who met him in Salzburg during their pilgrimage, called him a pleasant, considerate man with obvious musical talent and well familiar with his famous father's legacy. In 1826, Franz conducted Mozart's requiem at his stepfather Nissen's memorial service. He died in 1844.

PART II

Mozart

the

Man

Chapter 9

MOZART'S HEALTH

Assessing Mozart's personality and the relationships within his family are difficult. The legends about Mozart first appeared while he was still alive, beginning as stories that circulated as gossip about a man who became a celebrity in his own time. Then reports about him and about his sudden, early demise were published soon after his death. The first biography appeared just seven years after he died and a huge number of biographies, books and articles have been published since about him and his works.

Mozart's music not only continues to resonate with listeners, but engenders a fascination with the man who composed these weaving melodies, haunting and disturbing passages, serene and transcending airs. More than 200 years after his death, the outpouring of interest in his life and the scholarship of his music continues undiminished, and indeed may be increasing. The two hundredth anniversary of his death in 1991 led to the publication of several biographies and other studies and others continue to appear in the early years of the new millennium.

The sources that form the basis of scholarship about Mozart include his autographed works, the thematic catalogue of compositions that he compiled beginning in 1784, various publications of his works, and other surviving documents. Among these is extensive correspondence of the Mozart family, a diary kept by Mozart's sister and accounts of witnesses of the time, who included Mozart's widow, sister, colleagues, friends, pupils and other contemporaries. In addition to biographies and periodicals devoted to Mozart, his family and his music, important work includes studies of Mozart's handwriting by Wolfgang Plath and Alan Tyson's work on music paper types, which contributed to more correct dating of the compositions, and allowed insight into Mozart's compositional processes.

Despite all this, the task of trying to recreate exactly what transpired during Mozart's life and what he was like as a person is difficult because many accounts are simply not reliable. Those provided by various witnesses, including the family, may be affected by faulty memory of events, which in some cases, took place years or decades earlier and because the individuals, even in their correspondence, might not have been entirely truthful. After all, just as we do today, each had his or her own agenda.

Mozart's health has been a subject of extensive scholarship since shortly after his death. Probably the most credible work on this subject is the account of Dr. Anton Neumayr, a prominent Austrian physician, scientist and musician. In his book *Music and Medicine,* he assesses Mozart's illnesses and personality, and their potential relationship to his musicianship. His assessment is based on the Mozart family's correspondence, accounts of other witnesses, and contemporary publications. He discusses extensively the claims of other physicians and points out why a number of hypotheses are faulty in the light of the differences between the medical knowledge and terminology used in the eighteenth century and today. His conclusions are based on the best available information. Yet there is still room for other interpretations.

During the eighteenth century infant mortality was very high. Only two of Mozart's parents' seven children survived infancy. Similarly, only two of Mozart's six children survived. Yet, even in his immediate family, there was considerable variability. Among Leopold Mozart's eight siblings, only two died in infancy, while three brothers and three sisters survived into adulthood. Mozart's wife was among four of seven children who lived to between sixty and more than eighty years of age. The reasons for such variability are not clear. Periodic epidemics of infectious diseases may have played a part. Also, the custom of nursing newborns on water in which various foodstuffs were dissolved and denying them milk, a practice that was used by Mozart's parents, may have been an important contributing factor to the death of many infants. In such circumstances, the simple fact that Wolfgang and his sister survived suggests that they both had sound constitutions.

During their long travels, Leopold's children became ill many times and spent extended periods in bed. At times they were seriously ill, causing a real concern that they were about to succumb. An example is the typhoid fever with which both children fell ill in September 1765 in The Hague. First, Nannerl was so ill that she became delirious; the attending doctor had lost all hope and last rites were administered. Yet she hung on and after three weeks started to slowly improve. However, then Wolfgang contracted the disease. Leopold wrote in a letter of December 12th that the illness had "reduced him to such pitiable state for 4 weeks that he was not only absolutely unrecognizable but also nothing but skin and bones … on 1 December he was critical … then he lay for 8 days without saying a word." It was a month before the young prodigy could walk.

Other illnesses that Wolfgang contracted during the travels, besides common viral infections, included erythema nodosum, a complication of streptococcal infection, in Munich in 1762; recurrent tonsillitis, probably acute rheumatic fever in November 1766, smallpox in the fall of 1767, and likely viral hepatitis A, with jaundice, which was contracted during the second Italian trip in late 1771. Clearly, Mozart paid a price for his musical education and accomplishments during his travels. His life was in danger more than once, but he survived and there is no evidence that he suffered any longterm complications such as rheumatic heart disease or chronic nephritis.

By comparison, through most of his years in Vienna, Mozart was in good health. He had viral infections from which he recovered readily and there was an illness in 1784, which is thought by some to have been another streptococcal infection followed by glomerulonephritis, an inflammation of the kidneys. Over time, this condition may lead to kidney failure. However, the evidence indicates that the illness was more likely a bacterial or viral gastroenteritis, from which the composer recovered without further ill effect. Mozart was also ill in April 1787, but there is insufficient information to even speculate about the nature of the affliction. However, that bout of illness might have been one reason why Mozart did not travel to see his ailing father in Salzburg, who died a few weeks later.

In the years that followed, Mozart was frequently under considerable strain because of worries and efforts to extricate himself from financial predicaments, concerns about his wife's illnesses, and the stress of travels and work, which often entailed composing under the pressure of imminent deadlines. An example of the latter is the story about the composition of the overture to *Don Giovanni* in Prague in October 1787. The première was to take place the next day and, exhausted, Mozart kept falling asleep. As indicated earlier, he asked Constanze to keep waking him so he could continue to compose; the overture was finished just in time. Constanze confirmed this account in talking with Mary Novello, who visited her in 1829.

Not surprisingly, such stresses and worries led at times to periods of exhaustion and depression. There were weeks and even months during the last two years of the 1780s that Mozart spent in Vienna, when he composed little. Dr. Peter Davies, writing in *Mozart in Person: His Character and Health,* concluded that the composer suffered from a form of chronic bipolar disorder characterized by periods of excessively elevated and depressed moods that at times may result in mental breakdown or psychosis. H.C. Robbins Landon, one of the most prolific modern writers about Mozart, believed that such a disorder was likely responsible for compositions in minor keys; he provided a partial list of eighteen such works created between 1782 and 1791 and described them as disturbing, troubled, alarming and even dangerous(!). Yet, several of these "troubled" works were composed when Mozart would have been unlikely to be depressed, as they date from periods of triumphs, acclaim and happy, busy activity. Obviously minor keys do not of themselves signify a pathological state of mind.

In Mozart's case, they might have been variously written as a compositional challenge or may at times have reflected normal human sadness occasioned by a specific event. Among the latter, one could include the violin sonata in E Minor, composed around the time of the death of his mother in Paris; the string quartet in D Minor, created during Constanze's first labour, and the string quintet in G Minor, composed when Mozart was concerned about his father's seriously failing health. In these and other works, Mozart's music expresses human grief and sadness but with a beauty that exalts, rings true and tends to bring relief as it resonates in the inner being of the listener. H.C. Robbins Landon himself states, in response to those who have accused Mozart of heartlessness in composing the "musical joke", K. 522, soon after his father's death: "Such 'insights' reveal a lack of understanding concerning Mozart's way of thinking: when composing, he was always in a special world of his own, and his inner world had very little to do with external realities of life."

As Dr. Anton Neumayr points out, every person is subject to mood swings, with periods of elation and sadness. Mozart may have had a tendency to greater than average oscillations of mood, with periods of very high creativity and others of low activity, but these do not seem to be pathological. The ongoing stress of his financial matters, of family and work obligations, and the exertion to perfect his musical masterpieces, not surprisingly led to periods of extreme fatigue accompanied by a depressed mood during which he composed little. This was especially the case when Mozart was also trying to take care of his ailing wife.

Though it has been suggested that Mozart was ill with chronic kidney failure affecting him in his final year, Dr. Neumayr argues that he was basically in good health until the onset of his final illness in the latter half of November 1791. His conclusions are based on a number of considerations, including a healthy appetite, vigour, interest in his work, unflagging musical inspiration and compositional output. The final illness began with fever and exquisitely painful swelling and inflammation of the joints of his limbs, which made it almost impossible for him to move. The joint swelling and the resulting difficulty with movement have been erroneously interpreted by some writers to be generalized swelling of the body related to kidney failure or paralysis. However, the account of a physician and public health official, Dr. Guldener von Lobes, who was in close contact with Mozart's physicians and who viewed his body as a coroner, do not lend credence to these assertions.

The most likely diagnosis of Mozart's final illness is acute rheumatic fever with polyarthritis. This complication of streptococcal infection tends to occur in people with a history of previous episodes of such complications. Mozart was known to have had at least three such episodes. The condition led at times to very high fever, which was rapidly fatal, and associated with delirium into which Mozart slipped for a time before he died.

The contemporary use of emetics was likely responsible for his vomiting. The repeated bloodletting with which he was treated, in accordance with then-customary medical practice, and the vomiting would have contributed to his rapid demise (or perhaps even caused it!) by depleting his body and circulation of the large volume of fluid and blood needed to maintain hydration, blood volume and heart output. His doctor, when summoned in the evening, was reported by the biographer Nissen, who later married Mozart's widow, "to undertake the letting of the blood … whereupon his strength visibly ebbed and he fell unconscious and never came to again." Indeed, it is a sobering thought that Mozart might have survived had he not been treated by his physicians.

Mozart became ill on November 20, 1791 two days after attending the performance of his Masonic cantata "Laut verkünde unsere Freude". There is evidence that a febrile illness was prevalent in Vienna at that time and it is therefore possible that Mozart contracted a streptococcal infection at the performance. His previous episodes of complications of streptococcal infections would have made him more susceptible to it. Also, his immunity may have been weakened by stress.

Recent medical research provides evidence that negative emotions can intensify a variety of health threats, including those of an inflammatory nature. Though Mozart was in good spirits earlier in the fall, judging from his letters to Constanze, the great intensity with which he worked on the requiem and the court document of mid-November 1791, which showed a judgment against Mozart for a sum of 1,425 gulden owing to Prince Lichnowsky, could well have weakened his resolve and his defences, rendering

Joshua Stanton, 2005

This pen-and-ink portrait, by Canadian artist Joshua Stanton, is based on the 'unfinished portrait' that Constanze said looked most like her husband, as well as on a statue of the composer.

him more susceptible to infection and impairing his ability to recover.

The incident with Prince Lichnowsky, together with the very modest support from the imperial court of 800 gulden annually, likely awarded to dissuade him from leaving Vienna, underscore the impression that the Imperial Court and aristocracy, though appreciating and patronizing Mozart's art, failed to provide him with a stable environment. By extension, they might have contributed to shortening his life, thus resulting in an irreplaceable loss to mankind.

Chapter 10

FAMILY FINANCES

Mozart's father initially earned a modest living with a salary of 250 florins a year in Salzburg, which he supplemented by income from teaching and from the sales of his excellent *Violinschule* book. He was later promoted to the post of Vice-Kappelmeister and his salary was raised to 450 florins in 1779. The musical talent of his son opened the door to improvements in the financial situation of the family. The extensive travels when Wolfgang, and to a lesser extent his sister, were child prodigies were the first stage of this enterprise. The boy's amazing talent did indeed lead to a great success as royalty, nobility and the public were all captivated by his miraculous feats of musicianship. The family basked in the glories of these successes and Leopold particularly took pride in his son's accomplishments and the praise that he received on the wise education of his children. There were financial rewards from patrons in the form of currency and valuable gifts, as well as the earnings generated from numerous concerts, sale of compositions, and opera commissions.

It is very difficult, however, to determine the actual profits that resulted from the family's various tours, for they can only be inferred from available documents and are open to interpretation. The travelling was costly and fraught with dangers and difficulties, though the Court of the Archbishop supported some of the trips with modest grants.

The family often had to wait for days or even weeks for audiences with royalty and nobility, meanwhile using cash for lodgings and food. Also illnesses, which struck the children and Leopold, led to financial setbacks. What, for example, was the financial status of the family after it returned to Salzburg from its grand three-and-a-half-year European journey? While he was on the road, Leopold transmitted large sums of currency to Salzburg through his landlord and banker Johann Lorenz Hagenauer, with whom he maintained a detailed correspondence. It is not entirely clear whether the deposits were money that Leopold was accumulating as profit, or repayments on the advances that Hagenauer might have provided, and whether Leopold confided everything to Hagenauer. He might have been reluctant to divulge high earnings, lest such news jeopardize his standing with the archbishop, particularly because this particular journey was extremely long and during these years he provided no service to his employer. He was certainly anxious about the reception that might await him in Salzburg, though he reassured himself that his family reflected well on the court, which they represented.

When the family at last returned home, it was with many treasures: gold watches, snuffboxes, rings, and other items that a Salzburger who knew and visited the Mozarts after their return estimated as worth 12,000 florins. He also stated that Leopold brought other gifts and objects for resale for profit, but indicated that the journey was said to have cost 20,000 florins. In his biography, *Mozart: A Life*, Maynard Solomon estimated that Leopold probably cleared between 12,000 and 16,000 florins from the journey, although if his landlord was a partner and shared in the profits, the net gain would have been proportionately reduced.

Estimates suggest that Leopold accumulated a fortune equivalent to between twenty-five and fifty times his yearly salary. It is quite possible that this fortune would have remained largely intact through Leopold's careful management and investments plus the regular salary and other income generated by the father and son in Salzburg. There were also additional earnings from later trips that were offset in part by losses from the unsuccessful trip in 1768 and Wolfgang's trip to Paris in 1777–1778.

However, the accuracy of these estimates is uncertain, and one could also assume that the grand journey might have resulted in little or no financial gain. This view would explain Leopold's anxiety and exhortations during his son's trip to Paris, which began in 1777, when Wolfgang was twenty-one. In his letters, Leopold repeatedly reminded his son and his wife about the necessity of conserving funds, planning carefully and trying to earn as much as possible. He exerted pressure on Wolfgang by complaining about the debts the travellers were amassing, and informing him that his father's clothing "was in rags" and that he and his daughter could not even afford to attend the theatre. As the debts grew to more than 800 florins, the fifty-eight-year-old Leopold worried about his old age and his daughter's fate. Given those fears and worries, one might assume that the grand journey, and others that followed in the next decade, while resulting in fame, education and exposure for the Mozart family in many European countries, had been a financial failure. And if that was the case, if Leopold himself had been unable to succeed when travelling with his family, how could he expect that Wolfgang might be able to obtain a court appointment or bring home considerable earnings during the 1777–1779 trip?

The circumstances were very different during Mozart's tour as a young man than they had been when he and his sister toured as children. The fame and gratifying receptions during the earlier journeys had largely been occasioned by the amazing musical feats of child prodigies, who did not compete with or threaten local musicians. Now Wolfgang represented a rival who was travelling at a time of economic hardships occasioned by political events and limited court resources. Rivalry and professional jealousy had likely been at the root of the failure to perform Mozart's early opera *La finta semplice* in Vienna. And though they may have been justified, Leopold's indignation and complaints to the emperor might well have contributed to the Mozart's family reputation as difficult people, which could have further hindered Wolfgang's prospects as he sought appointments in various courts.

Another possible financial scenario assumes that the travels that Leopold undertook with his children allowed him to accumulate a fortune, which he was largely able to conserve throughout his life. This seems difficult to reconcile with his letters to Wolfgang and his wife about the family's precarious financial situation, with his detailed accounts of the debts he was obliged to undertake for the travellers, or with the constant pressure he exerted on Wolfgang to return home to help fulfill his family obligations, as the young composer lingered in Paris. Did Leopold make investments that tied up his capital? Or, fearing that Wolfgang's trip might fail, did he conceal a large "rainy day" fund as a reserve for his needs in old age and his daughter's needs should she not marry? After Wolfgang returned to Salzburg, the two salaries that the father and son commanded should have allowed Leopold to repay any debts he had undertaken by the time Wolfgang set out for Munich in 1780 to stage *Idomeneo*.

After Wolfgang broke with the archbishop and moved to Vienna, Leopold and Nannerl continued to live together in Salzburg supported by Leopold's salary and earnings from private business enterprises and teaching. Mozart's father took in an eleven-year-old live-in student from Munich, Heinrich Marchand, and later boarded Heinrich's sister as well. Nannerl likely also had earnings from teaching. It is known that she had earnings during her brother's 1777–1779 trip to Paris, for fifty florins of her savings served as collateral for Wolfgang's draw of funds. Wolfgang did not send his father money from Vienna. What he earned from his freelance efforts he needed for his own use and to support his wife and family.

It should be recalled that Leopold was not in favour of Wolfgang's marriage, for he felt that one should have a steady salary before starting a family; he also probably realized that he would not be able to count on any financial help from Wolfgang, once he married. He indicated to his son at the time that he should not expect any inheritance. On the other hand, Leopold was quite concerned about the fate of his daughter should he die, for she was still unmarried during Wolfgang's first few years in Vienna and dutifully shared her life with her father.

There is uncertainty surrounding the size and disposition of Leopold's estate after his death in 1787, as his will and other documents are missing. He left about 3,000 florins in currency and a large number of valuable items. After negotiations between Nannerl and her husband and Wolfgang, it was agreed that Wolfgang would receive 1,000 florins in cash, which he needed, while ceding the proceeds from the rest of the estate to his sister. A large number of items from the estate were auctioned soon after the agreement was reached; most of the items were sold, but some remained unsold and would have been retained by Nannerl, who also kept other objects that were not auctioned. Leopold had apparently bequeathed specific items to both children, but Wolfgang did not claim his.

Wolfgang corresponded with his sister about the disposition of their father's estate and continued sparingly thereafter. Mozart let her know about his court appointment. His last surviving letter to her was in 1788. He undoubtedly was very busy with work and family affairs, and in fact, said so in his correspondence to her. However, he showed no real concern for her after Leopold's death and made no effort to see her when he passed close to her home during his 1789 trip.

Biographer Ruth Halliwell has stated that sister and brother shared approximately equally in their father's estate, but that seems unlikely, as the estate consisted of about 3,000 florins in cash plus the proceeds of the auction of many valuable items and Wolfgang's share of the total was only 1,000 florins. Thus it appears that Nannerl ended up with a significantly larger proportion of her father's estate. She was able to make a deposit of 1,000 florins as savings in 1790. There is also a possibility that Leopold Mozart might have given some capital to his daughter before his death, although there is no direct evidence for such a transaction.

Nannerl's husband died in 1801. His estate realized more than 27,000 florins, which was to be divided among his six children, including the two borne to Nannerl. However, because he left his wife annual payments of 300 florins, the estate was tied up until arrangements were made a few years later to permit the children to obtain their inheritance, while assuring Nannerl her upkeep. Nannerl also inherited from the marriage a capital of more than 2,000 florins, according to the stipulations of the marriage contract and might have received a widow's pension from the Salzburg court of 300 florins. She was able to live quite comfortably. When her own daughter Jeanette, who was a singer and keyboard player, died at the age of sixteen in 1805, she left an estate of over 5,000 florins to her mother and brother Leopold. When Nannerl died in 1829, she left an estate with bonds and cash valued at close to 7,000 florins.

When Mozart first arrived in Vienna, he lived as a courtier of Archbishop Colloredo, but once he broke off with him, he had to start earning a living. His income came from payments he received from noble patrons at whose residences he was a sought after performer, as well as from teaching, commissions for operas and other compositions, benefit and subscription concerts, and from the sale of his compositions for publication. Beginning in 1787, he started drawing a salary of 800 gulden as a result of his appointment to the imperial court as Konzertmeister. His annual income is estimated to have varied between 1,500 and 2,000 florins in the lean years to above 5,000 annually. These figures put Mozart in a moderately high-income bracket.

The course of his financial affairs in Vienna is considered as that of increasing successes with earnings from numerous concerts peaking in the middle of the decade and then followed by a decline as the number of concerts dwindled, and other earnings did not adequately take up the slack. The decline was compounded by the expenses related to Constanze's illness and expensive cures in Baden in 1788 and 1791 and led to the series of letters seeking help from Puchberg.

However, Mozart's problems with debt seem to have begun soon after his marriage. In 1783, he wrote to his patron, Baroness von Waldstätten, asking her to bail him out when his loan was called sooner than he expected, and again in 1785 to the publisher Hoffmeister: "I turn to you with my problem and beg you to assist me with some money, which I need most urgently at present." While Mozart's frequent moves to new quarters in Vienna were probably undertaken largely to contain expenses, he continued to maintain a reasonably high standard of living, though apparently under increased financial pressures.

Again, caution is needed in considering this period. Though the decrease in concerts seemed to have taken place partly because of the war and general deterioration of the economy, some concerts likely did take place. In other words, the lack of evidence does not necessarily prove their absence, for there was little family correspondence during Mozart's last few years in Vienna following Leopold's death in 1787. And correspondence with his father had previously provided the most reliable documentation of

Mozart's performance activities.

Mozart continued to be active musically in Baron van Swieten's musical group in the latter part of the decade, and contrary to some statements, it is very likely there were concerts after Mozart composed his last three symphonies in 1788, during which they would have been performed. There was an attractive offer for a visit to England in 1790, which Mozart deferred but could have exercised later. As indicated earlier, in 1791 Mozart's fortunes seemed to be improving, as did his income. He obtained commissions for two operas and the requiem, he was composing more and there were apparently offers of substantial annual payments from abroad for providing compositions, exactly the type of arrangement that Mozart had sought for a long time.

It seems clear that Mozart was not very wise in handling his financial affairs and was living at times beyond his means, borrowing excessively against future earnings. He also made loans, some of which he lost when unscrupulous friends defaulted. He was ready, perhaps naïvely so, to help people in need; examples were taking pupils without asking for payments or lending 500 gulden to Anton Stadler in 1791. Because of his ongoing money problems, it has been suggested that Mozart was involved in gambling, but this is extremely unlikely, for no evidence for this exists.

However, it needs to be considered that Vienna was an expensive city to live in. Lodgings were particularly costly. There also were significant costs associated with Mozart's work, in the form of keyboard instruments, music paper, copyists' fees, and postage related to his correspondence with his father and sister, which often included sending his manuscripts and copies of his music. Since Mozart functioned in aristocratic circles and had contacts with the imperial court, he was obliged to spend considerable money on clothing. Despite such expenditures, he attended balls with his wife and gave at least one in his own quarters, acquired pets, a horse, a billiard table and a carriage; the last of these was used for his trip to Frankfurt in 1790. And Mozart's family employed a servant.

He not only paid for his wife's cures, but also enrolled his son Karl in an expensive boarding school. At the time of his death, he lived in a large apartment, with a billiards room, in the center of the city. Yet he took out a loan of 1,000 gulden against his possessions to consolidate his debts in 1790. It is not known why, in 1791, Mozart was pursuing an "N. N." (as it was referred to in his letters to his wife in Baden) to complete some crucial arrangement. Thus, though the state of his finances in the latter stages of his life is impossible to unravel and will likely remain a mystery, contrary to modern notions, he and his family did not live in poverty, but maintained a relatively high standard of living.

On his death, Mozart left debts of less than 1,000 florins. The total value of his possessions was assessed at less than 600 florins, but it was a normal practice at the time to undervalue the deceased person's possessions in order to save on estate taxes, which would burden the widow.

Mozart left his wife and two children with no established sources of income. He was not a member of the Society of Musicians, which provided pensions for widows, though he frequently provided music and performed at their benefit concerts. He was not a member because he never supplied a birth certificate. Yet he asked his father for a copy of his baptism. Did Leopold obtain it? Possibly Mozart's bitter break with the court in Salzburg had some bearing on this matter. Or Mozart may have been too busy with ongoing affairs to pursue the matter further; perhaps he was simply not concerned with the possibility of his death at a relatively young age.

After her husband's death Constanze had to fend for herself and her sons. She likely obtained some help from her family and probably considerable support and assistance from Mozart's affluent friends and patrons, particularly Baron van Swieten, who might have served as her advisor and assisted with the education of the children. Because Mozart had served as a court musician for less than ten years, his widow was not officially entitled to a pension. However, she petitioned the court, outlining her circumstances, and was granted a pension of one-third of Mozart's stipend, 266 florins annually.

Constanze energetically pursued various sources of income that became available. These included many benefit concerts, the sale of Mozart's manuscripts and copies of his compositions to patrons, including the German king, as well as to publishers. She fought hard for her rights to payments for Mozart's music from publishers, who tried to obtain it as cheaply as possible. The firm of Breitkopf & Härtel, one of the principal players, was hard to deal with. They were able to obtain Mozart's early music, written in Salzburg, from Nannerl without paying anything but the costs of copying and postage. At first, Nannerl seemed happy to contribute to the dissemination of her brother's music and to the biography the firm was planning to issue. She later found both the firm and her task difficult, as did Constanze. Slowly, Constanze's economic situation significantly improved. By 1797, six years after Mozart's death, she provided a loan of 3,600 florins to Josepha Duschek.

Chapter 11

Mozart's Personality

What can one conclude about Mozart's personality? Undoubedly its development would have been greatly influenced by his relationship with members of his immediate family and particularly with his father. As related earlier, despite their deep love, the heavy burden of knowing that he represented the main hope of the family for a better future must have weighed heavily on little Wolfgang. Later, the unresolved issues with his father, resulting from his decision to become independent and to marry, despite Leopold's opposition to both, affected him deeply and must have influenced how he felt, and in turn how he acted. Obviously, he was a complex human being with many facets. And though highly intelligent, this was not always evident on casual contact. Caroline Pichler, who knew Mozart, wrote:

> Mozart and Haydn, whom I knew well, were men who showed, in their personal associations with others, no other outstanding spiritual force and practically no sort of learning or higher culture. An everyday turn of mind, insipid jokes, and, as regards the former composer, a thoughtless way of life, were all they displayed in their associations … And yet what depths, what worlds of fantasy, harmony, melody, and emotion lay concealed behind these unprepossessing exteriors!

She would have had only a superficial contact with Mozart. Though music and composition were central to his life, he had other diverse interests. His library, according to the compilation of his possessions when he died, included books on philosophy, music, drama, poetry, geography, history, mathematics, travel, natural science, prose, religion, and fiction. Among them were works of Pietro Metastasio, awarded to him by Count Firmian at Milan in 1770 when he was just fourteen, and Molière's complete comedies, presented by Fridolin Weber as a farewell gift at Mannheim in 1778. Other books included the posthumous works of Frederick the Great, a biography of Emperor Joseph II, a dot book, a 1679 (Cologne) edition of the bible, and a book on learning English. Constanze told Vincent and Mary Novello that Mozart drew a little, manifested a talent for all the arts and was an admirer of nature and especially fond of flowers.

He enjoyed reading and was familiar with the works of Shakespeare. He knew several languages. A study by Catherine Morris Cox estimated the intelligence quotient (IQ) of eminent men and women who lived between 1450 and 1850, based largely on the degree of brightness and intelligence that they showed before the age of seventeen. Only about one per cent of people have an IQ greater than 135. Mozart's rating was 165, that of a genius, and similar to that of Copernicus and Darwin. Even taking into account the limitations of such extrapolations, the score fits with Mozart's superior capabilities.

From his father, Mozart acquired his broad interests, a deep religious faith and a profound distrust of clergy. He greatly enjoyed attending concerts and theatre performances, dancing, playing various games, and solving sophisticated puzzles. Progressive in his thinking, he embraced the ideas of Enlightment and maintained close relationships with members of different social classes. He particularly enjoyed gatherings at the homes of close friends as well as some of his patrons, among them the von Jacquins. Mozart and Constanze both had a close friendship with the talented Gottfried von Jacquin, in whose company they enjoyed serious music making, as well as jokes and horseplay.

Mozart also had several Jewish friends and was not influenced by the anti-Semitic views of the empress and some of the members of the court. He likely felt a kinship with the Jewish people and with members of bourgeoisie, who were beginning to make gains in the social structure of the Viennese community as a result of the Josephinian reforms. For example, Mozart's landlord in Vienna, Baron Raimund Wetzlar von Plankenstern, was a converted Jew. Mozart referred to him as an "honest" man and a "good and true friend". Wetzlar became godfather to Mozart's first child, who was named Raimund Leopold.

Though he was generous toward people he valued, Mozart could be critical and cutting to others that he considered superficial or whom he felt might threaten him. He loaned money to friends and refused payments for teaching his talented live-in pupil Nepomuk Hummel, but was often short of funds himself. In a letter written from Prague on October 15, 1787, he offered his pet dog to the father of his friend Gottfried von Jacquin. The old man had become fond of the dog, which Mozart left with the von Jacquins when he went to Prague.

Since he worked very hard composing and performing, it's remarkable that he was able to find time to participate in so many other activities. It is clear he enjoyed life: good food, fine clothing, playing games such as billiards and skittles, sexual pleasures, pets, horseback riding and walks in various parks and the Vienna woods. At times, he allowed himself to carry on to excess. He might have lived beyond his means, which contributed to his financial problems and strains on his family life. At the same time, he was devoted to his family. He sought, though unsuccessfully, to join a musicians' society, the membership in which would have provided his wife with a pension; took special care of his wife, and enrolled his son in an expensive boarding school.

Certainly there were rows between Wolfgang and Constanze on occasion, according to his sister-in-law, and some mutual jealousy. Whether or not he had extramarital affairs is not known, but several biographers think it unlikely. Their conclusions are based in large part on the evidence, obvious in his many letters, that Mozart loved his wife deeply and felt lost without her company. She shared his *joie de vivre*, participated in social events and high jinx escapades, was his confidant and ran the household.

This she did as she bore him six children during more than nine years of marriage. Thus she was pregnant for a total period of four-and-a-half years, and her chronic state of pregnancy must have contributed to her illnesses. It seems that it was she who secured an important loan in 1790 when Mozart was on his trip to Frankfurt, and she who organized the move to new, comfortable quarters, which must have been of considerable value to him when he returned. She had a considerable interest in music; Mozart played and sang his compositions to her as he was creating them. She liked fugues and encouraged Mozart to compose them. She had a pleasant voice and sang a soprano part in his mass in C Minor, K. 427, when it was performed during the visit to Salzburg in 1783, and in several benefit concerts after his death. After Mozart's death, Constanze worked hard and effectively to secure her family's financial position.

Mozart was sensitive and felt both joy and sadness intensely. This humanity is reflected in his music. His operas often focused on themes of forgiveness on the part of those in power, and on the weaknesses and foibles human beings in general—particularly the upper classes. He promoted the importance of women, which was progressive for his time, as well as the need for wisdom and self-assessment in human progress. As pointed out by Solomon, the music in Mozart's operas (for example in "The Magic Flute") and in other genres, has the capacity to lift the human spirit, particularly in times of hardship.

He composed from the age of five until disabled by his final illness, and seems to have lived immersed in music, as he explained in a letter to his father from Paris on July 31, 1778. "You know that I am, so to speak, soaked in music, that I am immersed in it all day long and that I love to plan works, study and meditate."

Chapter 12

Vignettes, Myths and Mysteries

Many anecdotes and stories reveal tantalizing glimpses of Mozart as a human being. Some appeared during his lifetime, while others came to light after his death. Though it's unlikely that much more will be forthcoming, the scholarship of more than two centuries has unravelled considerable information about Mozart. The work of William Stafford is particularly illuminating. Some of the stories have turned out to be baseless, others are well documented, but there remain a number of issues that cannot be objectively resolved and must, perhaps, remain as mysteries. This chapter deals with some of the vignettes that reveal certain aspects of Mozart's personality.

Mozart is said to have written the score of Gregorio Allegri's *Miserere* from memory after hearing it just once when in Italy in 1770. However, printed scores might have been available.

The circumstances of his admission to the academy were alluded to earlier. Contrary to his father's assertions, Mozart did not do very well on the difficult examination, but in consideration of his age–he was fourteen at the time—he was admitted after his work was corrected by Padre Martini.

Mozart's music was advanced for its time, often making it difficult to perform and sometimes to understand and enjoy by the public or even by professional musicians. Perhaps for these reasons, during his lifetime and for a considerable period after his death, his works were performed less often than the compositions of some of his contemporaries. Emperor Joseph II purportedly said to the composer after hearing the *Eintführung:* "Too beautiful for our ears, an enormous number of notes, dear Mozart."

While this is a good story, it first appeared more than fifteen years after it supposedly took place.

The subject of Mozart's relationships with women has been extensively debated. There is little doubt that he was full of strong sexual desires. If for no other reason, this is clear from the fact that during a marriage of close to nine-and-a-half years his wife gave birth to six children.

Young Mozart probably had little opportunity to sow his wild oats while in Salzburg, but was ready to explore relationships with the opposite sex during his trip in 1777. His liaison with his cousin Bäsle, which generated the famous letters filled with sexual connotations, seems unlikely to have been completely platonic. Clearly, she was more experienced than Mozart and continued to be sexually active after their time together in Munich and Salzburg. Many years after their youthful tête-a-tête, Bäsle gave birth to an illegitimate child, eliciting comments from Leopold and shock from Mozart's sister. It is clear from his letters that Mozart felt strongly about his cousin, but several biographers have claimed that "there is no evidence" for a sexual relationship between them. They apply the same reasoning to the possibilities of Mozart's extramarital relationships during his years in Vienna. But what possible evidence could there be? The absence of hard "evidence" does not rule out such possibilities.

There certainly appear to have been strains on Mozart's marriage, apparently with scenes of anger. His correspondence indicates the presence of mutual jealousies. During his trip to Germany in 1790, Mozart claims that the apparent lull in his correspondence, which probably concerned his wife, was due to several letters being lost. This seems unlikely, in part because there is little other documentation about the period when the letters were supposedly lost.

It has been suggested that Mozart was involved with the singer Josepha Duschek, and other women. Yet Duschek was a longtime friend of the family and after Mozart's death, Constanze lent her a considerable sum of money. There are also allegations about possible indiscretions when Constanze was in Baden and Mozart was working with the Schikaneder's troupe of actors and singers. These seem highly questionable. In fact, at the time, Mozart's letters to Constanze reveal, rather surprisingly, his jealousy of a wife in an advanced state of pregnancy.

His correspondence over the years leaves no doubt that he loved Constanze deeply, both as a life companion and as a sexual partner, but the question of his premarital and extramarital activities must remain another mystery.

Mozart's unfinished requiem and its eventual completion have generated a lot of print. There is evidence that some of the scoring was provided by two other pupils before Constanze asked Süssmayer to complete the score; she needed the fee that was to be paid upon the completion of the work. The idea that the patron who commissioned it might have been unwilling to pay for a composition by a lesser composer may be responsible for the stories of the notes that Süssmayer purportedly took from Mozart's desk, and of the instructions Mozart supposedly gave his pupil before he died. Both leave the impression that the work was essentially Mozart's.

The legend of the composer with a premonition of his own death, working feverishly on a requiem he believes may be for himself, evolved during the early nineteenth century. It may have been aided by Mozart's widow and her sister, who were with him during his final illness. Another story, of an informal rehearsal on the day of the composer's death, is highly suspect. If it had taken place, it would have been much earlier during his final illness, for as was discussed, Mozart was too ill to sing during his last day.

Was foul play involved in Mozart's death? There is no plausible material to support this idea and the story that he told his wife he thought he'd been poisoned seems improbable, given the accounts of his good spirits at the time. The notion that Salieri poisoned Mozart, which was based on some early rumours, was given impetus by the 1830 play *Mozart and Salieri* by Alexander Sergeievish Puskin and further propagated by an opera by Nikolai Andreievich Rimski-Korsakov and more recently by the film *Amadeus*, based on a play by Peter Shaffer.

Salieri, born six years before Mozart, became court composer and conductor of the Italian opera in Vienna in 1774. In 1788, he was appointed the court Kapellmeister. In Vienna at the time, he enjoyed great prestige; in modern times, however, he is mainly known because his name is invariably linked to that of Mozart and indeed, he may have opposed him occasionally and competed with him. At the same time, it does not appear that he intentionally tried to damage Mozart's work, despite the latter's complaints in his letters of perceived intrigues against him when his projects encountered delays.

That Salieri appreciated Mozart's music is evidenced by the fact that he conducted Mozart's masses and other works at the coronation of the new emperor, and must have given his approval for the revival of *Figaro* in Vienna in 1789. Mozart took Salieri and his wife to a performance of "The Magic Flute", where both raved about it. And after his death, Salieri tutored Mozart's sons. Nor do there seem to be grounds for the notion that Salieri, the Jews or the Masons poisoned Mozart, the last of these supposedly because he revealed Masonic secrets in "The Magic Flute".

Stafford discusses various myths of Mozart's personality that arose after his death. They include the eternal child, a difficult personality with little charitable appreciation of others and, just the opposite, a genius who was a social misfit, a social rebel, or a victim of circumstances and of intrigues. In *The Mozart Myths: A Critical Reassessment,* the author concludes that while it is difficult, if not impossible, to get a clear picture of the composer, he must have been a complex, multi-faceted person. Though a unique musical genius, he was at the same time, very human.

A statement by biographer Robert Gutman rings true:

> The decades I have passed studying Mozart have rich recompense in both acquaintance with and loving admiration for this affectionate man, an austere moralist of vital force, incisiveness, and strength of purpose who, though—like all—bearing the blame of faults and lapses, yet played his role in the human comedy with honor, engaging with grace the frustrations of his complicated existence: his goodness of heart, unaffected charm, winning ways, and self-humor run like gorgeous threads through its web.

Some of these characteristics also apply to the man who primarily influenced his development as a musician and as a person—his father, Leopold Mozart.

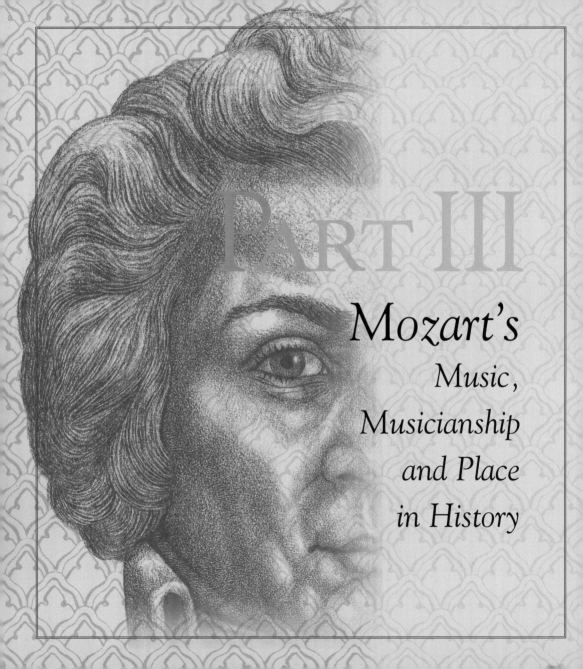

PART III

Mozart's
Music,
Musicianship
and Place
in History

Chapter 13

Music and Musicianship

Leopold Mozart had by far the most important role in his son's development as a musician. He tutored Mozart from early childhood with great care. He taught Wolfgang and his sister not only music, but other subjects as well. Young Wolfgang threw himself into many subjects, including arithmetic, but was most eager to learn to play music and to compose. He spent such long hours at the keyboard that, if not stopped and put to bed, would continue late into the night.

He had almost no formal schooling or musical training, other than that provided by his father, but Leopold meticulously assigned the boy work and carefully nurtured his development. This approach, combined with the child's musical genius, led to rapid progress. The isolated instances of tutoring by others included piano lessons with Johann Christian Bach and singing lessons from the castrato Giovanni Manzuoli, both during the year the family spent in London. Biographer Konrad Küster suggests that the singing lessons were related to the young Mozart's budding interest in vocal and operatic genres.

In Italy, there were sessions to study counterpoint with Father Martini, but wherever he went Mozart was always learning. He studied the works of his father and other composers, but he also absorbed simply by hearing. He attended numerous concerts, operas and other musical performances and because of his unique gift, was able to retain what he heard and assimilate it into his own musical style.

Following his son's rapid progress, Leopold encouraged Mozart to compose in the style of composers whose works they encountered in their travels, in part to ensure that the boy's own compositions would be well received by the local patrons and audiences. Thus Mozart easily acquired the ability to imitate the styles of others and stated this clearly in his later correspondence with his father. An example of this uncanny ability was the composition of two excellent duos for the violin and viola (K. 423 and K. 424), for his friend Michael Haydn, when Mozart visited Salzburg in 1783. Haydn had become ill and was unable to complete a commission of six such works for the Archbishop of Salzburg. Mozart's compositions, while full of beauty and sophistication, were crafted to be consistent with Haydn's style, making it difficult for the archbishop to recognize the deception.

The works of many masters influenced Mozart's music. These included German as well as Italian composers. While in London as a youngster, he was influenced by Johann Christian Bach and his concertos. He set Bach's piano sonatas with orchestral ritornellos and accompaniments as keyboard concertos (K. 107). And he was supposed to have said of Carl Philipp Emmanuel Bach: "He was the father of us all." While in Vienna, he was influenced by the compositions of Johann Sebastian Bach and Handel, which he arranged and prepared for performance during musical gatherings at Baron van Swieten's residence. He also studied J.S. Bach's manuscripts during his visit to Leipzig. Mozart became familiar with the pioneering compositions of Joseph Haydn in several genres, and was deeply influenced by them. And he was also influenced by the music of Haydn's younger brother, Michael, of Salzburg.

Mozart was clearly both a virtuoso and a superb composer. He became an excellent string player. He performed in the Court of the Archbishop and may have performed his violin concertos. However, he was known to have preferred the viola while playing chamber music. Yet, above all, he favoured the keyboard, and he became one of Europe's leading virtuosos on the clavier, performing his concertos and other compositions over many years, but particularly during his numerous concerts in Vienna. His widow told the Novellos that the organ was his favourite instrument and he was known to play it with great proficiency and virtuosity.

His musicality and genius allowed him to improvise with great facility, evoking a sense of wonder in his listeners and contributing to his fame. Reporting on a concert performance given by fifteen-year-old Mozart in Venice in 1771, the Hamburg newspaper *Staats und gelehrte Zeitung* stated, "An experienced musician gave him (Mozart) a fugue theme, which he worked out for more than an hour with such science, dexterity, harmony and proper attention to rhythm that even the greatest connoisseurs were astounded."

This ability is also revealed in a letter Mozart wrote to his father from Augsburg on October 23, 1777. During a concert at Holy Cross Monastery, Mozart had been given a theme and had performed various works on a small clavichord. He wrote:

> ... I put it [the theme] through its paces and in the middle (the fugue was in G Minor), I started off in the major key and played something quite lively, though in the same tempo; and after that the theme over again, but this time arseways. Finally it occurred to me, could I not use my lively tune as the theme for a fugue? I did not waste much time in asking, but did so at once, and it went as neatly as if Daser [a Salzburg tailor] had fitted it. The reception was staggering and phenomenal.

Mozart was preoccupied with music throughout his life. As he himself said, he was immersed in music all day long, planning works and composing. He was able to compose in his mind and pen the work on paper afterwards. He wrote on one occasion that while writing down a fugue that he already composed, he was composing in his mind an introductory *adagio*. This ability allowed him at times to play new compositions without having them written down, as was apparently the case during the performance of the sonata in B flat, K. 454, with the violinist Regina Strinasacchi in 1784.

Writing down his compositions was laborious and time consuming, however. And even composition itself was not always quick or easy, particularly when he was experimenting with new musical approaches; at times these proved to be a struggle. This was the case with his mature string quartets. The manuscripts of the quartets dedicated to Haydn show many erasures and corrections. And Mozart admitted to problems when composing the "Prussian quartets", which may have been started as a commission from the King of Prussia. Many unfinished fragments also bear witness to difficulties that Mozart encountered, particularly during the period of the "Bach crisis", when he was working on incorporating that master's techniques into his own style.

While composing in his mind, Mozart was able to carry on with daily life, operating, as one might put it today, on "automatic pilot". However, at times his behaviour did change, betraying his inner struggle to those who knew him. As quoted in Anton Neumayr's *Music and Medicine*, Mozart's brother-in-law, actor Joseph Lange, wrote in his 1808 memoirs:

> ... From his speech and actions, Mozart was never less to be recognized as a great man than when he was occupied with important work. Then he not only spoke in distracted, confused ways, but he would also make jokes of a kind one did not expect from him, indeed, he would even deliberately let his behavior go. All the while, he seemed not to be thinking or pondering on anything at all.

Lange believed that this odd behaviour was either a deliberate attempt to hide "his inner exertions under an external mask of frivolity" or to contrast "the heavenly ideas of his music ... with mundane everyday notions ..." This, he thought, might amuse the great composer with "a kind of self-irony".

Similarly, Neumayr quotes Mozart's sister-in-law Sophie Haibel as recalling in 1828:

> He was always good-humored, but ... very pensive, looking you right in the eye, giving answer to everything, whether sad or happy, and yet at the same time ... deep in thought, working on something completely apart. Even as he

was washing his hands in the morning, he would go back and forth in the room ...[or] tapping one heel against the other and being lost in thought.

These abilities—his remarkable facility for imitating the styles of others, combined with his unparalleled musical talents—enabled Mozart to absorb the approaches and techniques of others, and then, combining, modifying and improving upon them, arrive at his own ways of creating masterpieces in many genres.

An example of a composition that reflects his musical genius is the "Kegelstatt" trio in E flat Major, K. 498. Renowned musicologist Charles Rosen referred to it as "the great clarinet trio" and the work has an interesting history.

In scoring the trio for clarinet, viola and keyboard, Mozart departed from the pattern of piano trios of the time, in which a violin and cello supported the keyboard. Why did he decide to compose a work for such a unique instrumental set—one each from the wind, string and keyboard families? Replacing the violin with the clarinet and the cello with the viola presented both a challenge in balancing the parts of these instruments with their wide and overlapping registers, but at the same time opened an opportunity to juxtapose their contrasting timbres. Why did he do it?

The three instruments each had a special place in Mozart's heart. He was a great keyboard virtuoso and he became familiar with the clarinet during his early travels, for clarinets were not available in Salzburg at the time. He composed his best works for wind instruments (the *harmoniemusik*) in Vienna and clearly had a keen interest in the clarinet at the time the trio was composed. His compositions for clarinet solos are dedicated to or associated with his friend Anton Stadler, a virtuoso on the clarinet. In the previous seven months, he had used clarinets in three piano concertos, something he had not done in his previous piano concertos.

The viola, as stated earlier, was his favourite string instrument when playing string quartets and quintets. He apparently liked to be "in the middle of the harmony". Therefore it seems likely that he decided to replace the cello with the viola in the trio so that he himself could participate in its performance during a musical gathering at the von Jacquin residence, with his favourite piano pupil, Franziska von Jacquin, and his friend Anton Stadler on clarinet.

The "Keggelstatt" trio had been composed for Franziska, who was seventeen in 1786, and was likely first performed at the Wednesday musical on August 9th at her home.

How the trio was named may never be known, but it is known that nine days before, the words "while playing skittles" are written on the manuscript of a duo for French horns. Perhaps the nickname was shifted to the later composition; it's also conceivable that the ideas for the trio also came about while playing a game at the skittle alley or possibly on the grass court in the garden of the von Jacquin estate.

In addition to the unique instrumental set, the nature of the movements—*andante / menuetto e trio / rondeaux (allegretto)*— is unusual, with the minuet flanked by the outer movements, neither of which is in a fast tempo. All Mozart's mature piano trios essentially follow a fast / slow / fast pattern, as do the majority of Haydn's. The lengths of the movements— consecutively 129, 158 and 221 measures—also depart from the usual pattern, in which the first movement was generally the most important. Instead, Mozart shifts the weight and emphasis to culminate in the conclud- ing *rondeaux*. Einstein was moved to write,

> What is one to say of the Finale, a *rondo* that sings
> from beginning to end .... which then, gently triumphant, domi-
> nates the whole last part of the movement? How well Mozart
> now understands not only how to end a work, but how to close
> it, with a distillation of melodic and contrapuntal beauty that
> does not merely satisfy the listener but leaves him enchanted!

Roger Hellyer, writing in *The Mozart Compendium*, refers to the trio as "*unified* by one of the most innovative formal frameworks every devised", while Stanley Sadie calls it "among the *most unified in feeling* of Mozart's works" (my italics). How was this unification attained? The design binds all the movements together and each movement within itself.

The *andante* is unified by the second theme being derived from the first, by the continually recurring *grupetto* (a written out ornament) figure, and by the recurrent appearance of the transitional passage, which is related to the second motif of the first theme. The minuet features a similar rhythmic character of themes in both the minuet and the *trio*. The addition of a *coda* after the repeat of the minuet (a feature not seen in any of Mozart's minuets in his Viennese chamber works) provides a greater unified balance by the reappearance of the material of the *trio*. The *rondeaux*, besides its recurring refrains, is given greater internal cohesion through the use of part of the theme of the refrain in the 1st episode, and by the triumphant *coda* that masterfully integrates elements of the refrain and the melodic material of the episodes with brilliant *concertante* passages on the keyboard.

All three movements open with themes that begin with a sustained note and are followed by a series of short notes that rise in pitch and then fall. Passages with a sustained note followed by rising and falling short notes appear repeatedly in the rondeaux. Triplets first appear in the conclusion of the *andante*, then in the concluding phrases of both sections of the minuet, before figuring prominently as an agitated counter melody in the trio of the minuet. They then return in the 2nd and 3rd episodes of the final movement, binding the work together with the energetic, vivacious character of the triplet rhythm.

Though in a class of its own, the composition is a piano trio. In the latter part of the eighteenth century, piano trios had evolved from keyboard sonatas, and initially the string instruments had only a supporting role. Some early piano trios could be played as piano sonatas if string players were not available. In Mozart's piano trio K. 496 in G Major, composed a few weeks before the clarinet trio, both stringed instruments contributed substantially and assumed more independent roles.

The "Kegelstatt" trio can also be considered among works for wind instruments, with strings and/or keyboard. The trio and clarinet quintet that Mozart composed in 1789 paved the way for chamber works with clarinet by other composers in the nineteenth century, including Beethoven, Carl Maria von Weber, Robert Schumann, Johannes Brahms,

Maurice Ravel and Claude Debussy.

As a chamber composition of the eighteenth century, the "Kegelstatt" trio stands alone. The choice of clarinet and viola are unique as are the substantial contributions of both instruments. The piano exhibits the virtuosity reminiscent of Mozart's piano concertos, but its role is balanced by the music, which the composer gave to the other instruments. The clarinet has brilliant passages that carry the melodic line and the viola is not relegated to merely supporting the bass line of the keyboard, as the cello tended to do in early piano trios. Instead, it balances parts of the piano and clarinet with its own playing of thematic material, and provides important harmonic components and contrapuntal passages.

The clarinet trio epitomizes an important aspect of Mozart's approach to composition in that it departs from the norm and goes beyond the conventional. It is a piano trio, but much more than that. Mozart's chamber works of 1786 and thereafter have been referred to as having the character of "chamber concertos", in part because of the *concertante* style in the keyboard parts.

Mozart's compositional genius evolved in Vienna, as he composed his string quartets that he dedicated to Haydn between 1782 and 1785, his two piano quartets of 1785 and '86, and the piano concertos from 1784 to 1786. In the "Haydn" quartets, the parts of the second violin and the lower instruments acquired greater roles, while in the piano quartets the strings provide a solid balance for the keyboard. In the concertos, the piano part became increasingly balanced and contasted with the *harmonie* wind band, which played solo passages and thematic material supported or accompanied by the keyboard, and with the role of the strings. The "Kegelstatt" trio, with the brilliant *concertante* playing by the piano, and one wind and one string instrument, may be thought to represent a Mozart piano concerto reduced to its smallest instrumental common denominator.

Though Mozart's genius was fundamental to his accomplishments, the attainment of the supreme beauty and elegance of his compositions could have been achieved only by his deliberate planning, experimentation and commitment to hard work over his lifetime.

His musical style evolved from the simple early works of a precocious youngster, through the charming, bright concertos and orchestral works of extreme beauty of the young composer, to the highly complex mature music of the piano concertos, chamber works and operas of the mid-Viennese period. These later works—full of innovations and ethereal beauty with elements of sadness and turmoil—were followed by diverse compositions in many genres, a number of which displayed a simpler, more transparently elegant style. Perhaps at this stage of his life, Mozart felt the need for a purer elegance and beauty to balance the unsettling events in his life.

Even without the fragments, arrangements and additions, the list above adds up to more than 750, varying from short compositions and one-movement works to massive undertakings such as operas. Mozart was only one of many prolific composers, but the enduring appeal of his works is unique. Those that are a part of the active performance repertory more than 200 years after his death include more than half a dozen operas, a dozen or so symphonies, some twenty piano concertos, several concertos for other solo instruments; several divertimentos and serenades for orchestra, three serenades for wind ensembles (*harmoniemusik*), about ten piano sonatas and a similar number of violin sonatas, five piano trios, two piano quartets, two string duos, one string trio, ten string quartets, five string quintets, a half-dozen chamber works for wind instruments with strings, a quintet for winds and piano, and a clarinet trio. The active repertory also includes several concert arias, songs, and works of sacred music including the mass K. 427 and the requiem K. 626. Other compositions, including early works, can be at times heard at concerts or in radio broadcasts.

The larger proportion of his compositions, not surprisingly, was in the major keys. Among nearly thirty works in the minor keys, there

The Köchel catalogue can be consulted for a detailed listing of the composer's works in chronological order. This listing contains numbers K. 1 to K. 626, a remarkable output, given that Mozart was composing over a period of about thirty years, during a third of which he was a child. The listing that follows is based on the compilation in the Mozart Compendium, *edited by H.C. Robbins Landon.*

Operas and Musical Theatre—*eighteen, plus three operatic fragments*

Symphonies—*forty-one, plus a dozen others ascribed to Mozart, but with uncertain attribution*

Concertos
PIANO—*seven early works based on themes of other composers, twenty-three mature concertos and two separate* rondo *movements*

STRINGS—*five for violin, three separate movements for the violin, a concertone for two violins and* symphonie concertante *for violin and viola*

WINDS—*two for flute and one separate* adagio *movement, four for French horn, one each for bassoon, oboe, and clarinet, and one for flute and harp*

MISCELLANEOUS ORCHESTRAL (*divertimentos, cassations, serenades including several containing movements for solo violin or double bass*):— *twenty-five, plus fifteen marches, most to accompany the main works*

Dance and Ballet Music
BALLET—*three*   MINUETS—*ninety-five*
CONTRADANCES—*thirty-three*   GAVOTTES—*one*
GERMAN DANCES—*fifty-six*

Chamber Music
HARMONIEMUSIK

Winds
WINDS ALONE (*divertimentos, serenades and other several movement works*)—*seventeen*
WINDS WITH STRINGS AND PIANO—*nine*

Piano and Strings
PIANO AND VIOLIN—*twenty-eight*   PIANO TRIOS—*twelve*
PIANO QUARTETS—*two*

Strings Alone
DUOS AND TRIOS—*six*
QUARTETS—*twenty-three and one separate march*
QUINTETS—*six*

Piano Alone
SONATAS—*eighteen*
VARIATIONS—*sixteen*
MISCELLANEOUS *(minuets, fantasias*, rondos, *dances): thirty*

Piano Duets
SONATAS—*(one keyboard): five and one set of variations*
TWO KEYBOARDS—*one fugue and one sonata*

Mechanical Organ and Armonica: *five*

Sacred Music
MASSES AND REQUIEM—*twenty*

Miscellaneous
SHORT SACRED WORKS *(vocal and instrumental)—thirty-nine*
LITANIES AND VESPERS—*seven*
Oratorios, sacred dramas, cantatas: eight

Voice and Orchestra
ARIAS AND SCENES—*fifty-four*
DUETS AND ENSEMBLES—*four*

Songs, Vocal Ensembles and Canons
SONGS—*twenty-nine*
VOCAL ENSEMBLES—*eight*
CANONS—*thirty-four*

Arrangements and Additions
TRANSCRIPTIONS OF WORKS BY OTHER COMPOSERS—*fifteen*

Miscellaneous—*five*

Fragments and sketches—117

Lost—*forty-seven*

are symphonies, piano concertos, miscellaneous orchestral, chamber and sacred works. Only a few of these were composed during periods when Mozart might have been grieving or was greatly concerned.

Chapter 14

Assessing Mozart's Music

Mozart's music became popular during his lifetime. Large audiences of aristocracy, bourgeoisie and common people flocked to his concerts in Vienna and to the performances of his operas and other works throughout Europe, and many of his works were published. However, both listeners and performers found some of his music, with its plethora of musical ideas and new musical progressions and style, too difficult.

These difficulties, which seem to have been related to the complexity of his music, are the very qualities that have made such an indelible impression on the musicians and public of subsequent generations. The anecdote about the emperor's complaint that there were "too many notes" in his composition, whether true or not, accurately reflects how, at times, contemporary listeners found his music. The frustrations encountered by musicians when rehearsing some of his string quartets and the lack of success of his piano quartet subscription attest to the problems that both professional and amateur musicians had with some of his compositions. Despite high praise for the beauty and richness of his works, his contemporaries had difficulty dealing with them.

A discussion of the opera *Die Entführung* in a contemporary magazine stated:

> Next, the composer has been too loquacious with
> the wind instruments. Instead of only reinforcing the melody

where that is required, and supporting harmony as a whole, they often darken the former and confuse the latter, prevent simple, beautiful singing and disturb the singer's delivery ...

Similarly, the composer Carl Ditters von Dittersdorf, an older contemporary of Mozart, remarked of his compositions:

Indisputably he is a genius, and I have yet to find any composer possessing such an astonishing richness of ideas. I could wish that [he was] not so spendthrift with them. He does not allow the hearer to pause for breath; for the moment one relishes a beautiful idea, along comes another, driving away the first, and immediately that leads on to yet another, so that in the end one can retain none of these real beauties in the memory.

The music lovers of the eighteenth century did not have the opportunity to hear compositions as frequently as modern audiences have, beginning with the era of recordings in the first half of the twentieth century. During his lifetime, some of Mozart's works were performed many times soon after their composition, but many others were not. For example the *Eintführung* was often performed in Vienna and elsewhere during Mozart's life; but *Idomeneo*, arguably the greatest *opera seria* of its century, enjoyed only a few performances. The latter undoubtedly was also the case with many of Mozart's chamber compositions.

Interestingly, Joseph Haydn encountered a similar problem at times during his earlier employment at Esterháza, the estate of Count Johann Esterházy. He wrote in a letter in 1776:

... I only wonder why it is that the otherwise so intelligent ... gentlemen have no middle ground in their criticism of my compositions, for in one week they raise me to the stars, in another they hammer me 60 fathoms into the ground, and all that without explaining why.

In response to such criticisms and perhaps as a result of a hint from his employer, Haydn adjusted in the direction of music that was light, lively and pleasing. His music became widely accepted and was more popular during the nineteenth century than that of Mozart, who was reluctant to compromise and alter his musical ideas.

Haydn himself considered Mozart to be a supreme composer, as is evident by his statement to Leopold Mozart when he visited his son in Vienna. While one might argue that Haydn was being excessively kind or generous while speaking to the father of the composer, his other statements attest to his very high regard for Mozart. For example, in a letter written in December 1787 to Franz Roth in Prague, and published in Franz Xaver Niemetschek's 1798 biography, Haydn wrote:

> If I could only impress on the soul of every friend of music, and on high personages in particular, how inimitable are Mozart's works, how musically intelligent, how extraordinarily sensitive! (for this is how I understand them, how I feel them)—why then the nations would vie with each other to possess such a jewel within their frontiers. Prague should hold him fast—but should reward him too, for without this, the history of great geniuses is sad indeed, and gives but little encouragement to posterity to further exertions; and unfortunately this is why so many promising intellects fall by the wayside. It enrages me to think that this incomparable Mozart is not yet engaged by some imperial or royal court!

Neumayr also quotes Haydn as declaring to a music dealer in England about Mozart: "Friends often flatter me that I have some talent, but he stood far above me."

Mozart's contemporary, composer Giovanni Paisiello wrote: "I showed it [the fugue in G from the first of Mozart's "Haydn quartets"] to the [celebrated composer Gaetano] Latilla, who pronounced it to be a masterly piece: ... [and stated] ... 'This is the most magnificent piece of music I ever saw in my life' ..."

Schubert, as quoted by Solomon, wrote in his diary on June 13, 1816: "As from afar the magic notes of Mozart's music still gently haunt me … They show us in the darkness of this life a bright, clear, lovely distance, for which we hope with confidence. O Mozart, immortal Mozart, oh how endlessly many such comforting perceptions of a brighter and better life hast thou brought to our souls!"

Beethoven purportedly cried to a friend after hearing Mozart's piano concerto in C Minor, "Cramer, Cramer! We shall never be able to compose anything like it!" He also remarked, "I have always reckoned myself among the greatest admirers of Mozart, and shall do so till the day of my death."

Johannes Brahms said: "Each number in Mozart's *Figaro* is a miracle to me; I simply cannot conceive how someone can create something so perfect; it has never been done since, not even by Beethoven."

Mozart's music influenced and was highly regarded by many other composers including Fryderyk Chopin. Peter Tschaikowsky composed a suite, *Mozartiana*; composer and Pulitzer Prize winner Michael Colgrass created "A letter from Mozart" and a number of other composers, including Beethoven, Franz Liszt, Joseph Gelinek, Fernendo Sor and Max Reger transcribed, arranged or composed variations based on Mozart's music.

Chapter 15

Mozart's Place in History

Mozart's place in the development of Western music is central, in that he combined techniques and approaches of several of his predecessors and contemporaries in ways that transcended and surpassed them, and thereby paved the way for subsequent evolution during the nineteenth century. As stated earlier, particularly in his string quartets and symphonies, Mozart was greatly influenced by the works of the elder Haydn. He modelled his chamber and symphonic works by following in the footsteps of Haydn, but put his own stamp on them. In turn, Mozart's "Haydn quartets" influenced the subsequent compositions of the older master.

Mozart blazed the trail for Beethoven and other composers who followed. When young Beethoven was setting out for Vienna, his supporter Count Waldstein, wrote to him: "With the help of assiduous labour you shall receive Mozart's spirit from Haydn's hands." The music of Mozart's somber *rondo* in A Minor, K. 511, for piano contains hints of romanticism and of the style later made famous by Chopin.

Mozart introduced many new approaches in the construction of compositions in various genres, and in the way he developed his works, introducing into them more abundant melodic ideas, changing the weights of various sections of movements, and unifying his compositions. Twentieth century Austrian-American composer Arnold Schoenberg asknowledged that he had learned primarily from Bach and Mozart, and listed the inequality of phrase length, coordination of heterogeneous characters in forming a thematic unity, and the art of introduction, transition and forming of subsidiary ideas among the many specific items he learned from Mozart.

Mozart's quintet for keyboard and four single wind instruments, K. 452, led Beethoven and other composers to follow suit. He was one of the first to compose piano quartets by the addition of viola to the standard piano trio. His success in this genre led other composers to follow in his footsteps including Beethoven, Felix Mendelssohn, Johannes Brahms, Anton Dvorzák and Gabriel Fauré.

It is also remarkable that Mozart's achievements and influence in vocal music and opera were comparable with his instrumental works of various forms, an accomplishment attained by few other great masters. When he felt it fit his purpose, he composed using previously developed forms to perfection. Yet when he felt the music needed it, he went beyond the conventional, incorporating numerous motifs, asymmetries, instabilities and disorders. These enhanced the beauty of the music, making it ephemeral and poignant, thus reflecting the inner human experience. It is possible that the difficulties, emotional struggles and heartaches that Mozart experienced combined with his genius, intellect and hard work to create music that is unmatched in poignancy and beauty.

These views are reflected in the following statements by other authorities: musicologist Cliff Eisen wrote of the touching quality of Mozart's music: "[It] has an unmatched abundance of ideas, motifs, melodies, and inventions. Yet [it] does not break down, [but] stays cohesive and leaves listener satisfied. That is Mozart's genius—Mozart's music expresses human experience and speaks to the listener. Mozart was very human, with positive characteristics though he had a share of suffering."

The biographer Gutman wrote, "Mozart (like Goethe) would raise German eclecticism to commanding heights; he blended the Baroque and Rococo with Storm and Stress [*Sturm und Drang*, that tumultuous German movement dotting on eccentricity, surprise and exaggerated individualism] ... and partook of Italian songfulness, Gallic wit and German melancholy."

Cliff Eisen and Stanley Sadie relate that when conductor Otto Klemperer was asked to list his favourite composers, Mozart's name was not mentioned. When asked about it, Klemperer apparently replied, "Oh,

I thought you meant the others."

Whether true or not, the anecdote illustrates that there is little doubt about the superior importance of Mozart, especially as a composer of operas, concertos, symphonies and chamber music. He seems to be regarded as the supreme composer.

In *Mozart: A Musical Biography*, Konrad Küster wrote, "Mozart went beyond the accepted contemporary limits laid down in the musical rulebook, not in details alone but comprehensively ... Mozart had reached what ... was his 'late' style, at the age of 30—which is a preposterous statement in itself. The thought of what might have happened if he had lived to 60 takes the breath away."

The reference to his death as an "irreplaceable loss" by the *Wiener Zeitung* the day after Mozart died was certainly most appropriate. Indeed, Mozart's music is imbued with his unique genius and universal humanity and towers over the realm of Western music.

Though considerably larger than it was when he grew up there, Mozart would undoubtedly recognize Salzburg today, for the city has retained its graceful character.

EPILOGUE

Mozart's music is one of the greatest gifts to mankind as it continues to appeal to connoisseurs and amateurs alike. Its unique human element seems to resonate in the inner being of performers and listeners. Author Marcia Davenport writes, "Mozart gives ever more impressive proof that there really is immortality. First in his music; then in the fascination that he holds for people of all persuasions and ages."

The German soprano Dorothea Roschmann, talking about singing Mozart operas, said that "Singing his music is among the hardest things I can imagine, because it's this combination of simplicity—that is, of complete control—and complete transparency and complete emotion."

His music encompasses the whole range of emotions: simple beauty, exuberant joy, romance and tenderness, foreboding and dark moods, and inner emotional struggles. Probably foremost is the feeling of longing. It seems to be the longing for happiness, beauty and bliss, which humans can experience but fleetingly.

In his book *The Disciplined Mind*, educator Howard Gardner stated that education should be concerned with the pursuit and understanding of Truth, Beauty and Morality. He used an example of each; for beauty, he chose a trio from *Le nozze di Figaro*. There is some evidence that listening to music, and perhaps especially to that of Mozart, may improve human functioning and health. In September 2004, the 15th International Congress on Care of the Terminally Ill in Montreal featured a panel discussion on the healing power of music and an all-Mozart concert by Les

Violons du Roy, with the guest conductor, Trevor Pinnock, vocal soloists and La Chapelle de Québec choir.

CBC broadcaster Allan McPhee once said, "A day without Mozart is like a day without sunshine".

Robert Stanfield, a one-time leader of the Conservative Party of Canada, when asked whether he regretted never becoming a prime minister, replied "Sure, it would have been wonderful to have served as Prime Minister, but how much greater a thing would it have been to have composed one of Mozart's piano sonatas?"

George Bernard Shaw wrote, "There is nothing better in art than Mozart's best."

And Goethe, an obvious fan, wrote in *Italienische Reise*, "All our endeavours ... to confine ourselves to what is simple and limited were lost when Mozart appeared. *Die Eintführung aus dem Serail* conquered all."

Mozart has been called "an angel sent by God to Earth" and, comparing him to one of his successors, it was said "When angels play for God, they play Beethoven; when they play for themselves, they play Mozart."

Appendix

These fifty Mozart masterpieces were chosen arbitrarily for readers who are about to embark on the exploration of the wonders of his music. The list intentionally includes works of various genres, but necessarily omits numerous wonderful compositions, as even a complement of a hundred works would do.

Operas:

"The Marriage of Figaro", K. 492
Così fan tutte, K. 588
"The Magic Flute", K. 620

Arias:

"Ruhe sanft", from *Zaide*, K. 344
"A questo seno ... Or che il cielo", K. 374

Symphonies:

In E flat Major, K. 543
In G Minor, K. 550
In C Major, K. 551—"Jupiter"

Concertos:

Piano:

In E flat Major, K. 271—"Jenamy"
In G Major, K. 453
In D Minor, K. 466
In C Major, K. 467

In A Major, K. 488
In C Minor, K. 491
In B flat Major, K. 595

Other instruments:

Violin, in G Major, K. 216
Violin, in A Major, K. 219
Violin and viola, *sinfonia concertante* in E flat Major, K. 364
Bassoon in B flat Major, K. 191
Clarinet in A Major, K. 622

Miscellaneous Instrumental:

Serenade in D Major, K. 320, ("Posthorn")
Wind serenade (*Parthia*) in C Minor, K. 388

Chamber Music:

Solo piano:

Sonata in A Minor, K. 310
Fantasia in C Minor, K. 475
Rondo in A Minor, K. 511
Sonata in B flat Major K. 538
Sonata in C Major, K. 545

Piano and violin:

Sonata in D Major, K. 306
Sonata in B flat Major, K. 454

Piano trios:

In B flat Major, K. 502
In E Major, K. 542

PIANO QUARTETS:

In G Minor, K. 478
In E flat Major, K. 493

STRING DUO:

In B flat Major, K. 424

STRING TRIO:

In E flat Major, K. 563

STRING QUARTETS:

In D Minor, K. 421
In B flat Major, K. 458—"Hunt"
In C Major, K. 465—"Dissonance"
In D Major, K 499—"Hoffmeister
In B flat Major, K. 589—"Second "Prussian"

STRING QUINTETS:

In C Major, K. 515
In G Minor, K. 516
In D Major, K. 593
In E flat Major, K. 614

WIND AND OTHER INSTRUMENTS:

Clarinet trio in E flat Major, K. 498—"Kegelstatt"
Clarinet quintet in A Major, K. 581

SACRED MUSIC:

Motet "Exultate jubilate" in F Major, K. 165
Missa in C Minor, K. 427
Motet "Ave verum corpus" in D Major, K. 618
Requiem in D Minor, K. 626

GLOSSARY

This short glossary of musical terms is provided to assist readers not familiar with musical terminology.

CADENZA—a passage in the style of brilliant improvisation, generally near the end of a solo composition or movement

CODA—a concluding section falling outside the basic structure of the composition, and added in order to heighten the impression of finality

CONCERTANTE—brilliant rapid instrumental parts, frequently found in concertos

CHROMATIC, CHROMATICISM—the use of raised or lowered notes, instead of the normal degrees of the scale, for example c-d-d#-e in the key of C Major

DOMINANT—the fifth degree of the scale, so called because of its "dominating" position in melody as well as in harmony; for example g in the key of C Major

ENHARMONIC—pertains to a change in the notation and function of a single pitch, for example from e flat to d sharp

FUGUE—a polyphonic composition based on a theme, which, stated at the beginning in one part or voice, is then taken up by other parts and reappears throughout the piece

KEY (scale)—The "main note" of a composition and by extension all notes related to that central note. In the case of compositions, which consist of several movements, the key designation refers at least to the first movement

176

MAJOR, MINOR—referring to the two basic scales of music since about 1700; the major and the minor scales are distinguished by the third degree (a whole tone in a major scale, a half tone in a minor scale)

MINUET—a graceful seventeenth-century French dance in moderate triple time

MODULATION—the change of key within a composition

OBBLIGATO—with reference to an instrument or to a part that is essential and cannot be omitted. Often referring to an instrumental solo accompanying a vocal part, for example in some of Mozart's arias

SCHERZO—a movement that evolved from the minuet. May be of a jesting type (the word denotes a joke in Italian). Often took the place of a minuet, for example in the second or third movement of a composition, such as a symphony. Developed further by Beethoven, Chopin and other composers

SEMIQUAVER—a sixteenth note

SONATA FORM—a form frequently used for single, often first, movements of a sonata, a symphony or other compositions. It consists essentially of three sections called exposition, development and recapitulation

SUBDOMINANT—the fourth degree of the scale, i.e.: f in the key of C Major

RONDO/RONDEAU—an instrumental form of the seventeenth century, consisting of a recurring section, the "refrain", played in alternation with three or more varying sections called episodes or couplets

TONIC—the first and main note of a key, for example c in C Major

TRIO—a group of three performers, also the music they perform. For example a piano trio, which is usually music for piano, violin and cello, is most common. Also, the name of the middle section of a minuet or a *scherzo*

TRIPLET—a group of three notes to be played within one beat of a measure

Bibliography

Listed in chronological order:

Caroline Pichler, *Denkwürdigkeiten aus meinem Leben 1769 – 1843*, (München: bei Goerg Müller, 1914).

Catherine Morris Cox, *The early mental traits of three hundred geniuses*: *Genetic studies of geniuses* (Vol. II), (Stanford University Press, 1926).

"A Mozart Pilgrimmage", Being the Travel Diaries of Vincent & Mary Novello in the year 1829, Nerina Medici di Marignano, transcriber and compiler, (London, Novello and Company Ltd, 1955).

Marcia Davenport, *Mozart*, (New York, Avon Books, 1932, 1956).

Willi Apel, Ralph T. Daniels, *The Harvard Brief Dictionary of Music*, (New York, Washington Square Press, 1960).

Frederich Kerst, *Beethoven: The Man and the Artist, as Revealed in His Own Words* (Dover Publications, Inc. New York, 1964).

Stuart Andrews, *Eighteenth-Century Europe: the 1680s to 1815,* (Longmans, Green and Co., London.

Alfred Einstein, *MOZART: His Character, His Work*, (New York: Oxford University Press, 1965).

Otto Erich Deutsch, *Mozart, a Documentary Biography,* (Stanford, California, Stanford University Press, 1965).

Emily Anderson, *The Letters of Mozart And of His Family*, Second ed., Volumes I and II, (London: MacMillan; New York: St Martin's Press, 1938/1966).

Michael Levey, *The Life and Death of Mozart*, (London, Weidenfeld and Nicolson, 1971).

Paul Roussel, *Mozart Seen Through 50 Masterpieces*, (Cambridge, Ontario: Habitex Books, 1976).

W·A·MOZART

SONATAS·FOR·THE·PIANOFORTE·

EDITED AND REVISED BY
RICHARD EPSTEIN

NOTE: The numbers in ( ) are the corresponding numbers in the Lebert edition.
*Accompaniments for Second Piano by Edvard Grieg for Nos. 3, 4, 5 and 18 may be found in Schirmer's Library, Vols. 1440-1-2-3, respectively.

G. SCHIRMER, Inc. NEW YORK

This composition, Price, 50 cents, in U. S. A.

Stanly Sadie, *The New Grove Mozart*, (New York: W. W. Norton, 1982).

HC Robbins Landon, *Mozart: The Golden Years 1781-1791*, (London: Thames and Hudson, 1989).

Peter J. Davies, *Mozart in Person, His Character and Health*, (New York, Greenwood Press, 1989).

The Compleat Mozart, N. Zaslaw, W Cowdery, eds, (New York: W.W. Norton & Co., 1990).

The Mozart Compendium, H.C. Robbins Landon, ed., (New York: Schirmer Books, 1990).

Mozart Briefe und Aufzeichnungen, Wilhelm A. Bauer, Otto Erich Deutsch eds., (Kassel , Bärenreiter, 1990-1991).

Cliff Eisen, *New MOZART Documents: A Supplement to O.E. Deutsch's Documentary Biography* (Stanford, California, Stanford University Press, 1991).

William Stafford, *The Mozart Myths, A Critical Reassessment* (London, Stanford University Press, 1991).

Anton Neumayr, *Music & Medicine*; Haydn, Mozart, Beethoven, Schubert (Bloomington, Illinois, Medi-Ed, 1994).

Bruce A. Brown, *W. A. Mozart: Così fan tutte*, (New York, Cambridge University Press, 1995).

H.C. Robbins Landon, *The Mozart Essays*, (London: Thomas and Hudson, 1995).

Maynard Solomon, *Mozart, A Life*, (New York: Harper Collins, 1995).

Konrad Küster, *Mozart: A Musical Biography*, (1991; translated by Mary Whitthall, Oxford: Oxford University Press, 1996).

A Mozart Diary, compiled by P. Dimond (Westport, Conn., Greenwood Press, 1997).

D.G. Campbell, *The Mozart Effect: Tapping the power of music to heal the body, strengthen the mind, and unlock the creative spirit*, (New York: Avon Books, 1997).

Charles Rosen, *The Classical Style: Haydn, Mozart, Beethoven*, expanded ed. (New York: W.W. Norton, 1997).

Roy Porter, *The greatest benefit to mankind: A medical history of humanity,* (New York, W.W. Norton & Company, 1997).

Ruth Halliwell, *The Mozart Family: Four Lives in a Social Context,* (Oxford, Clarendon Press, 1998).

Howard Gardner, *The Disciplined Mind: What All Students Should Understand,* (New York: Simon & Schuster, 1999).

Robert W. Gutman, *Mozart, A Cultural Biography*, (New York, Harcourt Brace & Co., 1999).

Cliff Eisen and Stanley Sadie, *The New Grove Mozart*, (London. MacMillan Publishers, 2002).

JK Kiecolt-Glaser, l McGuire, TF Robles, R Glaser, "Psychoneuroimmunology and psycho-somatic medicine: back to the future," *Psychosomatic Medicine,* 64 :15–28, 2002.

JK Kiecolt-Glaser, L McGuire, TF Robles, R Glaser, "Emotions, Morbidity, and Morality: New Perspectives from Psychoneuroimmunology," *Annual Review Psychology*, 53: 83–107, 2002.

Stefan Carter, "Concerning the Death of Leopold Mozart", (Kassel Bärenreiter, Henning Bay and Johanna Senigl, eds.), in *Mozartjahrbuch*, pp. 259-264, 2003/04.

Michael Lorenz, Jenamy-Concerto program notes, 2004, quoted in the *Newsletter of the Mozart Society of America,* IX (1), January 27, 2005.

Dr. Stefan Carter

Born and brought up in Warsaw, Poland, Stefan Andrew Carter miraculously survived the horrors of World War II and immigrated to Winnipeg in 1948. He enrolled in the University of Manitoba and graduated with M.Sc. and M.D. degrees in 1954. He did postgraduate training in cardiovascular function and vascular disease in Winnipeg, New York and the Mayo Clinic.

In 1958, he returned to Winnipeg to join the staff at the Faculty of Medicine of the University of Manitoba in the Departments of Physiology and later Medicine.

Over a period of forty years his teaching about cardiovascular function was combined with research and clinical work. The results of his research were presented at national and international meetings and led to numerous publications in refereed journals, reviews and book chapters. Throughout this time, he was a staff member at St. Boniface Hospital and director of its Vascular Laboratory. In 2003, he was a recipient of the St. Boniface Heart Care Award.

His extracurricular activities include talking about his experiences in World War II to high school and university students, and are centred on his family and music. He married Emilee N. Horn, an artist and teacher in the blackboard jungle of New York. They are proud of their sons, Dr. Joel W. Carter, an ER and palliative care physician with an interest in the therapeutic role of storytelling, and Andrew T. Carter, a choreographer and theatre director.

Dr. Carter's interest in music originated with his family in Poland, and continued in Canada as an amateur on period intruments—the recorder and viola da gamba—and recently the clarinet. His passionate interest in Mozart has led to a study over a number of years and recently to an essay on the death of Leopold Mozart, published in the *Mozartjahrbuch* ("Mozart Year Book"), as well as to this book.